Raymond F. Jones was born in Salt Lake City in 1915. His first story was published in 1941. As well as many short stories, he has written several highly regarded novels (both adult and juvenile) of which *This Island Earth* and *Renaissance* are probably the best known.

By the same author

RAYMOND F. JONES

This Island Earth

GraftonBooks

A Division of HarperCollinsPublishers

GraftonBooks
A Division of HarperCollins*Publishers*
77–85 Fulham Palace Road,
Hammersmith, London W6 8JB

Published by Grafton Books 1991
9 8 7 6 5 4 3 2 1

First published in Great Britain by
TV Boardman 1954

This Island Earth is partially based upon material originally
published in *Thrilling Wonder Stories*, and copyrighted by
Standard Magazines, Inc.
Copyright © Raymond F. Jones 1952

ISBN 0-586-21050-4

Printed and bound in Great Britain by
Collins, Glasgow

Set in Times

for David

1

The offices of Joe Wilson, purchasing agent for Ryberg Instrument Corporation, looked out over the company's private landing field. Joe stood by the window now, wishing they didn't, because it was an eternal reminder that he'd once had hopes of becoming an engineer instead of an office flunky.

He saw the silver test ship of the radio lab level off at bullet speed, circle once and land. That would be Cal Meacham, Joe thought. Nobody but a radio engineer would fly an airplane that way.

He chomped irritably on his cigar and turned away. From his desk he picked up a letter and read it through slowly for the fourth time. It was in answer to an order he had placed for condensers for Cal's hot transmitter job – Cal's stuff was always hot.

Dear Mr Wilson:
We were pleased to receive your order of the 8th for samples of our XC-109 condenser. However, we find that our present catalogue lists no such item nor did we ever carry it.

We are, therefore, substituting the AB-619 model, a high-voltage oil-filled transmitting-type condenser. As you specified, it is rated at 10,000 volts with 100% safety factor and has 4 mf. capacity.

We trust these will meet with your approval and that we may look forward to receiving your production order for these items. It is needless, of course, to remind you that we manufacture a complete line of electronic components. We would be glad to furnish samples of any items from our stock which might interest you.

Respectfully yours
A. G. Archmanter·
Electronic Service – Unit 16

Joe Wilson put the letter down slowly and took up the box of beads that had come with it.

He picked up one bead by a lead wire sticking out of it. The bead was about a quarter of an inch in diameter and there seemed to be a smaller concentric shell inside. Between the two was some reddish liquid. Another wire connected to the inner shell, but for the life of him Joe couldn't see how that inner wire came through the outer shell.

It made him dizzy to concentrate on the spot where it came through. The spot seemed to shift and move.

'Ten thousand volts!' he muttered. 'Four mikes!'

He tossed the bead back into the box. Cal would be hotter than the transmitter job when he saw these.

Joe heard the door of his secretary's office open and glanced through the glass panel. Cal Meacham burst in with a breeze that ruffled the letters on Joe's desk.

'See that landing I made, Joe? Markus says I ought to be able to get my license to fly that crate in another week.'

'I'll bet he added "if you live that long."'

'Just because you don't recognize a hot pilot when you see one – what are you so glum about, anyway? And what's happened to those condensers we ordered three days ago? This job's *hot*.'

Joe held out the letter silently. Cal scanned the page and flipped it back to the desk.

'We'll try them out. Give me an order and I'll pick them up from Receiving on my way to the lab.'

'They aren't in Receiving. They came in the envelope with the letter.'

'What are you talking about? How could they send sixteen mikes of ten kv condensers in an envelope?'

Joe held up one of the beads by a wire. 'Guaranteed one hundred percent voltage safety factor.'

'What screwball's idea of a joke is this? Did you call Receiving?'

Joe nodded. 'I checked *good*. These beads are all that came.'

Cal grasped one by the lead wire and held it up to the light. He saw the faint internal structure that Joe had puzzled over.

'It *would* be funny if that's what these things actually were, wouldn't it?' he said.

'You could build a fifty kw transmitter in a suitcase, provided you had other corresponding components.'

Cal dropped the rest of the beads in his shirt pocket. 'Call them on the teletype. Tell them this job is plenty hot and we've got to have those condensers right away.'

'What are you going to do with the beads?'

'I might put ten thousand volts across them and see how long it takes to melt them down. See if you can find out who pulled this gag.'

For the rest of the morning Cal checked over the antenna on his new ground transmitter, which wasn't putting out power the way it should. He forgot about the glass beads until late in the afternoon.

Then, as he bent his head down into the framework of the set, one of the sharp leads of the alleged condensers stuck through his shirt.

He jerked sharply and bumped his head on the iron framework. He cursed the refractory transmitter, the missing condensers and the practical joker who had sent the beads. He pulled the things out of his shirt pocket and was about to hurl them across the room.

But a quirk of curiosity halted his hand in midair. Slowly he lowered it and looked again at the beads that seemed to glare at him like eyes in the palm of his hand.

He called across the lab to a junior engineer. 'Hey,

Max, come here. Put these things on voltage breakdown and see what happens.'

'Sure.' The junior engineer rolled them over in his palm. 'What are they?'

'Just some gadgets we got for test. I forgot about them until now.'

He resumed checking the transmitter. Crazy notion, that. As if the beads actually were anything but glass beads. There was only one thing that kept him from forgetting the whole matter. It was the way that one wire seemed to slide around on the bead when you looked at it –

In about five minutes Max was back. 'I shot one of your gadgets all to pieces. It held up until thirty-three thousand volts – and not a microamp of leakage. Whatever they are they're *good*. Want to blow the rest?'

Cal turned slowly. He wondered if Max were in on the gag, too. 'A few hundred volts would jump right around the glass from wire to wire without bothering to go through!'

'That's what the meter read.'

'Come on,' said Cal. 'Let's check the capacity.'

First he tried another on voltage test. He watched it behind the glass shield as he advanced the voltage in steps of five kv. The bead held at thirty – and vanished at thirty-five.

His lips compressed tightly, Cal took the third bead to a standard capacity bridge. He adjusted the plugs until it balanced – at just four microfarads.

Max's eyes were slightly popped. 'Four mikes – they *can't* be!'

'No, they can't possibly be, can they?'

Back in the Purchasing Office Cal found Joe Wilson sitting morosely at the desk, staring at a yellow strip of teletype paper.

'Just the man I'm looking for,' said Joe. 'I called the Continental Electric and they said – '

'I don't care what they said.' Cal laid the remaining beads on the desk in front of Joe. 'Those are four-mike condensers that don't break down until more than thirty thousand volts. They're everything Continental said they were and more. Where did they get them? Last time I was over there Simon Forrest was in charge of the condenser department. He never – '

'Will you let me tell you?' Joe interrupted. 'They didn't come from Continental. Continental says no order for condensers has been received from here in the last six weeks. I sent a reorder by TWX.'

'I don't want their order then. I want more of these!' Cal held up a bead. 'But where did they come from if not from Continental?'

'That's what I want to know.'

'What letterhead came with these? Let's see it again.'

'It just says, "Electronic Service – Unit Sixteen." I thought that was some subsection of Continental. There's no address on it.'

Cal looked intently at the sheet of paper. 'You're sure this came back in answer to an order you sent Continental?'

Wearily, Joe flipped over a file. 'There's the duplicate of the order I sent.'

'Continental always was a screwball outfit, but they must be trying to top themselves. Write them again. Give the reference on this letter. Order a gross of these condensers. While you're at it ask for a new catalogue. Ours may be obsolete. I'd like to see what else they list besides condensers.'

'Okay,' said Joe. 'But I tell you Continental says they didn't even get our order.'

'I suppose Santa Claus sent these condensers!'

11

Three days later Cal was still ironing the bugs out of his transmitter when Joe Wilson called again.

'I just got the condensers – and the catalogue! For the love of Pete, get up here and take a look at it!'

'A whole gross of condensers? That's what I'm interested in.'

'Yes – and billed to us for thirty cents apiece.'

Cal hung up and walked out towards the Purchasing Office. Thirty cents apiece, he thought. If that outfit should go into the business of radio instruments they could probably sell a radio compass for five bucks.

He found Joe alone, an inch thick manufacturer's catalogue open on the desk in front of him.

'Did this come from Continental?' said Cal.

Joe shook his head and turned over the front cover. It merely said, *Electronic Service – Unit 16*.

'We send letters to Continental and stuff comes back,' said Cal. 'Somebody over there must know about this! What's so exciting about the catalogue?'

Joe arched his eyebrows. 'Ever hear of a catherimine tube? One with an endiom complex of plus four, which guarantees it to be the best of its kind on the market?'

'What kind of gibberish is that?'

'I dunno, but this outfit sells them for sixteen dollars each.' Joe tossed the catalogue across the desk. 'This is absolutely the cockeyedest thing I ever saw. If you hadn't told me those beads were condensers I'd say somebody had gone to a lot of work to pull a pretty elaborate gag. But the condensers were real – and here's a hundred and forty-four more of them.'

He picked up a little card with the beads neatly mounted in small holes. 'Somebody made these. A pretty doggoned smart somebody, I'd say – but I don't think it was Continental.'

Cal was slowly thumbing through the book. Besides the

gibberish describing unfamiliar pieces of electronic equipment there was something else gnawing at his mind. Then he grasped it. He rubbed a page of the catalogue between his fingers and thumb.

'Joe, this stuff isn't even paper.'

'I know. Try to tear it.'

Cal's fingers merely slipped away. 'That's as tough as sheet iron!'

'Whoever this Electronic Service outfit is, they've got some pretty bright engineers.'

'Bright engineers! This thing reflects a whole electronic culture completely foreign to ours. If it had come from Mars it couldn't be more foreign.'

Cal turned the pages, paused to read a description of a *Volterator incorporating an electron sorter based on entirely new principles*. The picture of the thing looked like a cross between a miniature hot air furnace and a backyard incinerator and it sold for six hundred dollars.

He came to an inner dividing cover at the center of the catalogue. *For the first time*, the center cover announced, *Electronic Service – Unit 16 offers a complete line of interocitor components. In the following pages you will find complete descriptions of components which reflect the most modern engineering advances known to interocitor engineers*.

'Ever hear of an interocitor?'

'Sounds like something a surgeon would use to remove gallstones.'

'Maybe we should order a kit of parts and build one up,' said Cal whimsically.

'That would be like a power engineer trying to build a high-power communications receiver from the *Amateur's Handbook* catalogue section.'

'Maybe it could be done.' Cal stared at the pages before him. 'Do you realize what this means – the extent of the knowledge and electronic culture behind this? It exists right here around us somewhere.'

'Maybe some little group of engineers that doesn't believe in exchanging information through the IRE and so on? But are they over at Continental? If so why all the beating about the bush telling us they didn't get our order?'

'It looks bigger than that,' said Cal doubtfully. 'Regardless, we know their mail goes through Continental.'

'What are you going to do about it?'

'Do? I'm going to find out who they are! Mind if I take this catalogue along?'

'It's all right with me,' said Joe. 'I don't know what it's all about. I'm no engineer – just a dumb purchasing agent around this joint.'

'For some things you can be thankful,' said Cal.

2

The suburb of Mason was a small, moderately concentrated industrial center. Besides Ryberg Instrument there were Eastern Tool and Machine Company, the Metalcrafters, a small die-making plant, and a stapling-machine factory.

This concentration of small industry in the suburb made for an equally concentrated social order of engineers and their families. Most of them did have families but Cal Meacham was not yet among these.

He had been a bachelor for all of his thirty-five years and it looked as if he were going to stay that way. He admitted that he got lonely sometimes but considered it well worth it when he heard Frank Staley up and about at two A.M. in the apartment above his, coaxing the new baby into something resembling silence.

He ate at the company cafeteria and went home to ponder the incredible catalogue that Joe Wilson had obtained. He couldn't understand how such developments could have been kept quiet. And now, why were they being so prosaically announced in an ordinary manufacturer's catalogue? It made absolutely no sense whatever.

He settled down in his easy chair with the catalogue propped on his lap. The section on interocitor components held the greatest fascination for him.

But there was not a single clue as to what the interocitor was, its function or its purpose. To judge from the list of components, however, and some of the sub-assemblies that were shown, it was a terrifically complex piece of equipment.

He picked up the latest copy of the *Amateur's Handbook* and thumbed through the catalogue section. Joe had been right in comparing the job of assembling an interocitor to that of a power engineer trying to build a radio from the *Handbook* catalogue. How much indication would there be to a power engineer as to the purposes of the radio components in the catalogue?

Practically none. He gave up the speculation. He had already made up his mind to go to Continental and find out what this was all about. He *had* to know more about this stuff.

At seven there was a knock on his door. He found Frank Staley and two other engineers from upstairs standing in the hall.

'The wives are having a gabfest,' said Frank. 'How about a little poker?'

'Sure, I could use a little spending money this week. But are you guys sure you can stand the loss?'

'Ha, loss, he says,' said Frank. 'Shall we tell him how hot we are tonight, boys?'

'Let him find out the hard way,' said Edmunds, one of Eastern's top mechanical engineers.

By nine-thirty Cal had found out the hard way. Even at the diminutive stakes they allowed themselves he was forty-five dollars in the hole.

He threw in his final hand. 'That's all for tonight. You can afford to lose your lunch money for a couple of months but nobody will make mine up at home if I can't buy it at the plant.'

Edmunds leaned back in his chair and laughed. 'I told you we were hot tonight. You look about as glum as Peters, our purchasing agent did today. I had him order some special gears from some outfit a while back and they sent him two perfectly smooth wheels.

'He was about ready to hit the ceiling when he discovered that one wheel rolled against the other would drive it. He couldn't figure it out. Neither could I when I saw it. So I mounted them on shafts and put a motor on one and a pony brake on the other.

'Believe it or not those things would transfer any horsepower I could use and I had up to three hundred and fifty. There was perfect transfer without measurable slippage or backlash. The craziest thing you ever saw.'

Like some familiar song in another language Edmunds' story sent a wave of almost frightening recognition through Cal. While Staley and Larsen, the third engineer, listened with polite disbelief, Cal sat in utter stillness, knowing it was all true. He thought of the strange catalogue in his bookcase.

'Did you find out where the gears came from?' he asked.

'No, but we intend to. Believe me, if we can find out the secret of those wheels it's going to revolutionize the entire science of mechanical engineering. They didn't come from the place we ordered them from. We know that much. They came from some place called merely "Mechanical Service – Unit Eight." No address. Whoever they are they must be geniuses besides being screwball business people.'

Electronic Service – Unit 16, Mechanical Service – Unit 8 – they must be bigger than he had supposed, Cal thought.

He went out to the little kitchenette to mix some drinks. From the other room he heard Larsen calling Edmunds a triple-dyed liar. Two perfectly smooth wheels couldn't transmit power of that order merely by friction.

'I didn't say it was friction,' Edmunds was saying. 'It was something *else* – we don't know what.'

Something *else*, Cal thought. Couldn't Edmunds see

17

the significance of such wheels? They were as evident of a foreign kind of mechanical culture as the condensers were evidence of a foreign electronic culture.

He went up to the Continental plant the next day, his hopes of finding the solution there considerably dimmed. His old friend, Simon Forrest, was still in charge of condenser development.

He showed Simon the bead and Simon said, 'What kind of a gadget is that?'

'A four-mike condenser. You sent it to us. I want to know more about it.' Cal watched the engineer's face closely.

Simon shook his head as he took the bead. 'You're crazy! A four-mike condenser – we never sent you anything like this!'

He knew Simon was telling the truth.

It was Edmund's story of the toothless gears that made it easier for Cal to accept the fact that the condensers and catalogue had not come from Continental. This he decided during the ride home.

But *where* were the engineers responsible for this stuff? *Why* was it impossible to locate them? Mail reached Electronic Service through Continental. He wondered about Mechanical Service. Had Eastern received a catalogue of foreign mechanical components?

Regardless of the fantastic nature of the task, he made up his mind to do what he had suggested at first. He was going to attempt the construction of an interocitor.

But *could* it be done? Now that it was a determined course, the problem had to be analyzed further. In the catalogue were one hundred and six separate components. He knew it was not simply a matter of ordering one of each and putting them together.

That would be like ordering one tuning condenser, one

coil, one tube and so on and expecting to build a super-het from them. In the interocitor there would be multiples of some parts, and different electrical values.

And, finally, if he ever got the thing working how would he know if it were performing properly or not?

He quit debating the pros and cons. He had known from the moment he first looked through the catalogue that he was going to try.

He went directly to the Purchasing Office instead of his lab the next morning. Through the glass panels of the outer room he saw Joe Wilson sitting at his desk, his face over a shoe box, staring with an intent and agonized frown.

Cal grinned to himself. It was hard to tell when Joe's mugging was real or not, but he couldn't imagine him sitting there doing it without an audience.

Cal opened the door quietly, and then he caught a glimpse of the contents of the box. It was *wriggling*. He scowled, too.

'What have you got now? An earthworm farm?'

Joe looked up, his face still wearing a bewildered and distant expression. 'Oh, hello, Cal. This is a tumbling barrel.'

The contents of the box looked like a mass of tiny black worms in perpetual erratic motion. 'What's the gag this time? That box of worms doesn't look much like a tumbling barrel.'

'It would – if they were metallic worms and just walked around the metal parts that needed tumbling.'

'This isn't another Electronics Service – 16 product, is it?'

'No. Metalcrafters sent over this sample. Wanted to know if they could sell us any for our mechanical department. The idea is that you just dump whatever needs tumbling into a box of this compound, strain it out in a few minutes and your polishing job is done.'

'What makes the stuff wiggle?'

'That's the secret that Metalcrafters won't tell.'

'Order five hundred pounds of it,' said Cal suddenly. 'Call them on the phone and tell them we can use it this afternoon.'

'What's the big idea? *You* can't use it.'

'Try it.'

Dubiously, Joe contacted the order department of Metalcrafters. After a moment he hung up. 'They say that due to unexpected technological difficulties in production they are not accepting orders for earlier than thirty day delivery.'

'The crazy dopes! They won't get it in thirty days or thirty months.'

'What are you talking about?'

'Where do you think they got this stuff? *They* didn't discover it. They got it the same way we got these condensers and they're hoping to cash in on it before they even know what it is. As if they could figure it out in thirty days!'

Then he told Joe about the gears of Edmunds.

'This begins to look like more than accident,' said Joe.

Cal nodded slowly. 'Samples of products of an incredible technology were apparently missent to three of the industrial plants here in Mason. But I wonder how many times it has happened in other places. It almost looks like a pattern of some sort.'

'But who's sending it all and how and why? Who developed this stuff? It couldn't be done on a shoestring, you know. That stuff smells of big money spent in development labs. Those condensers must have cost a half million, I'll bet.'

'Make out an order for me,' said Cal. 'Charge it to my

project. There's enough surplus to stand it. I'll take the rap if anybody snoops.'

'What do you want?'

'Send it to Continental as before. Just say you want one complete set of components as required for the construction of a single interocitor model. That may get me the right number of duplicate parts unless I get crossed up by something I'm not thinking of.'

Joe's eyebrows shot up. 'You're going to try to build one by the Chinese method?'

'The Chinese method would be simple,' said Cal. 'They take a finished cake and reconstruct it. If I had a finished interocitor I'd gladly tackle *that*. This is going to be built by the Cal Meacham original catalogue method.'

He worked overtime for the next couple of days to beat out the bugs in the airline ground transmitter and finally turned it over to the production department for processing. There'd still be a lot of work on it because production wouldn't like some of the complex sub-assemblies he'd been forced to design – but he'd have time for the interocitor stuff between jobs.

After two weeks he was almost certain that something had gone wrong and they had lost contact with the mysterious supplier. Then Receiving called him and said that fourteen crates had just been delivered for him.

Fourteen crates seemed a reasonable number but he hadn't been prepared for the size of them. They stood seven feet high and were no smaller than four by five feet in cross section.

As he saw them standing on the receiving platform Cal visioned cost sheets with astronomical figures on them. What had he got himself into?

He cleared out one of his screen rooms and ordered the stuff brought in.

In some attempt to classify the components he laid like

units together upon the benches around the room. There were plumbing units of seemingly senseless configuration, glass envelopes with innards that looked like nothing he had ever seen in a vacuum tube before. There were boxes containing hundreds of small parts which he supposed must be resistances or condensers – though his memory concerning the glass beads made him cautious about jumping to conclusions regarding anything.

After three hours, the last of the crates had been unpacked and the rubbish carted away. Cal Meacham was left alone in the midst of four thousand, eight hundred and ninety-six – he'd kept a tally of them – unfamiliar gadgets of unknown purposes and characteristics. And he hoped to assemble them into a complete whole – of equally unknown purposes.

He sat down on a lab stool and regarded the stacks of components. In his lap rested the single guide through this impossible maze – the catalogue.

3

That evening he had dinner at the plant cafeteria, then returned to the now empty lab. It would take all his nights for months to come.

He hoped there wouldn't be too much curiosity about his project but he could see little chance of keeping it entirely under cover. Most of all he was concerned with keeping Billingsworth, the chief engineer, from complaining about it. This was *big* for a sideline project.

It was obvious that certain parts constituted a framework for the assembly. He gathered these together and set them up tentatively to get some idea of the size and shape of the finished device.

One thing stood out at once. There was a cube of glass, sixteen inches on a side, filled with a complex mass of elements. Twenty-three terminals were on the outside of the cube. One side of it was coated as if it were a screen. One of the framework panels had an opening exactly the right size to accommodate the face of the cube.

That narrowed the utility of the device, Cal thought. It provided an observer with some kind of intelligence which was viewed in graphic or pictorial form as with a cathode-ray tube.

But the complexity of the cube's elements and the multiple leads indicated another necessity. He would have to order duplicates of many parts because these would have to be dissected to destruction in order to determine electrical function.

Nearly all the tubes fell into this classification and he began listing these parts so that Joe could reorder.

He then turned to familiarizing himself with the catalogue name of each part and establishing possible functions from the descriptions and specifications given.

Slowly, through the early morning hours pieces fitted together as if the whole thing were a majestic jigsaw puzzle. At three A.M. Cal locked the screen room and went home for a few hours' sleep, elated by the clues he had discovered.

He was in at eight again and went to Joe's office.

'I see your stuff came,' said Joe. 'I wanted to come down, but I thought you'd like to work it out alone for a while.'

Cal understood Joe's frustrations. 'Come down anytime. There's something I'd like you to do. On the crates the stuff came in there was an address of a warehouse in Philadelphia. I wrote it down here. Could you get one of the salesmen to see what kind of a place it is when he's through there? I'd rather not have him know I'm interested. This may be a lead.'

'Sure. I think the Sales Office has a regular trip through there next week. I'll see who's on it. What have you found out?'

'Not too much. The thing has a screen for viewing but no clue as to what might be viewed. There's a piece of equipment referred to as a *planetary generator* that seems to be a sort of central unit, something like the oscillator of a transmitter, perhaps. It was mounted in a support that seems to call for mounting on the main frame members.

'This gives me an important dimension so I can finish the framework. But there're about four hundred and ninety terminals – more or less – on that planetary generator. That's what's got me buffaloed but good. These parts seem to be interchangeable in different circuits, otherwise they might be marked for wiring.

24

'The catalogue refers to various elements, which are named, and gives electrical values for them – but I can't find out which elements are which without tearing into sealed units. So here's a reorder on all the parts I may have to open up.'

Joe glanced at it. 'Know what that first shipment cost?'

'Don't tell me it cleaned my project out?'

'They billed us this morning for twenty-eight hundred dollars.'

Cal whistled softly. 'It should have been nearer twenty-eight thousand.'

'Say, Cal, why can't we track this outfit down through the patent office? There must be patents on the stuff.'

'There's not a patent number on anything. I've already looked.'

'Then let's ask them to send us either the number or copies of the patents on some of these things. They wouldn't distribute unpatented items like this, surely. They'd be worth a fortune.'

'All right. Put it in the letter with your reorder. I don't think it will do much good.'

Cal worked impatiently through the morning on consultations with the Production Department regarding his transmitter. After lunch he returned to the interocitor. He decided against opening any of the tubes. If anything should happen to their precarious contact with the supplier before they located him –

He began work on identification of the tube elements. Fortunately the catalogue writers had put in all voltage and current data. But there were new units that made no sense to Cal – *albion factors, inverse reduction index, scattering efficiency.*

Slowly he went ahead. Filaments were easy but some of the tubes had nothing resembling filaments or cathodes.

When he applied test voltages he didn't know whether anything was happening or not.

Gradually he found out. There was one casual sketch showing a catherimine tube inside a field-generating coil. That gave him a clue to a whole new principle of operation.

After six days he was able to connect proper voltages to more than half his tubes and get the correct responses as indicated by catalogue specifications. With that much information available he was able to go ahead and construct the entire power supply.

Then Joe called him one afternoon. 'Hey, Cal! Have you busted any of those tubes yet?'

'No. Why?'

'Don't! They're getting mad or something. They aren't going to send the reorder we asked for and they didn't answer about patents on the stuff. Besides, that address in Philadelphia turned out to be a dud.

'Cramer, the salesman who looked it up, says there's nothing there but an old warehouse that hasn't been used for years. Cal, who can these guys be? I'm beginning to not like the smell of this business.'

'Read me their letter.'

'"Dear Mr Wilson," they say, "We cannot understand the necessity of the large amount of reorder which you have submitted to us. We trust that the equipment was not broken or damaged in transit. However, if this is the case please return the damaged parts and we will gladly order replacements for you. Otherwise we fear that, due to the present shortage of interocitor equipment, it will be necessary to return your order unfilled.

'"Please feel free to call upon us at any time. If you find it possible to function under present circumstances will you please contact us by interocitor at your earliest convenience and we will discuss the matter further."'

'What was that last line?' Cal asked.

' – "contact us by interocitor – "'

'That's the one! That shows us what the apparatus is – a communication device.'

'But from where to where and from whom to whom?'

'That's what I intend to find out!'

They weren't going to let him open up the tubes or other sealed parts. Cal arranged for an X-ray and fluoroscope equipment to obtain some notion of the interior construction of the tubes he could not otherwise analyze. He could trace the terminals back to their internal connections and be fairly sure of not burning things up with improper voltages to the elements.

Besides the power supply, the entire framework with the planetary generator was erected and a bank of eighteen catherimine tubes was fed by it. The output of these went to a nightmare arrangement of plumbing that included unbelievable flares and spirals. Again he found prealigned mounting holes that enabled him to fit most of the plumbing together with only casual reference to the catalogue.

Growing within him was the feeling that the whole thing was some intricately designed puzzle and that clues were deliberately placed there for anyone who would look.

Then one of the catherimine tubes rolled off a table and shattered on the floor.

Cal thought afterwards that he must have stared at the shards for a full five minutes before he moved. He wondered if the whole project were lying there in that shattered heap.

Gently, with tweezers, he picked out the complex tube elements and laid them on a bed of dustless packing material. Then he called Joe.

'Get off another letter to Continental – airmail,' he

said. 'Ask if we can get a catherimine replacement. I just dropped one.'

'Aren't you going to send the pieces along as they asked?'

'No. I'm not taking any chances with what I've got. Tell them the remains will be forwarded immediately if they can send a replacement.'

'OK. Mind if I come down tonight and look things over?'

'Not at all.'

It was a little before five when Joe Wilson finally entered the screen room. He looked around and whistled softly. 'Looks like you're making something out of this, after all.'

A neat row of panels nearly fifteen feet long stretched along the center of the room. In the framework behind was a nightmarish assemblage of gadgets and leads. Joe took in the significance of the hundreds of leads that were in place.

'Manufacturers' catalogues are my line,' he said. 'I see hundreds of them every year. I get so I can almost tell the inside layout just by the cover.

'Catalogue writers aren't very smart, you know. They're mostly forty-fifty-dollar-a-week kids that come out of college with a smattering of journalism but are too dumb to do much about it. So they end up writing catalogues.

'And no catalogue I ever saw would enable you to do this!'

Cal shrugged. 'You never saw a catalogue like this before.'

'I don't think it's a catalogue.'

'What do you think it is?'

'An instruction book. Somebody wanted you to put this together.'

Cal laughed. 'Why would anyone deliberately plant this stuff so that I would assemble it?'

'Do *you* think it's just a catalogue?'

Cal stopped laughing. 'All right, but I still think it's crazy. There *are* things in it that wouldn't be necessary if it were only a catalogue. For instance, this catherimine tube listing.

'It says that with the deflector grid in a four-thousand-gauss field the accelerator plate current will be forty mils. Well, it doesn't matter whether it's in a field or not.

'But that's the only place in the whole book that indicates the normal operation of the tube is in this particular field. There were a bunch of coils with no designation except that they are static field coils.

'On the basis of that one clue I put the tubes and coils together and found an explanation of the unknown "albion factor" that I've been looking for. It's that way all along. You're right about catalogue writers in general, but the guy that cooked this one up was a genius.

'Yet I still can't quite force myself to the conclusion that I was *supposed* to put this thing together, that I was deliberately led into it.'

'Couldn't it be some sort of Trojan Horse gadget?'

'I don't see how it could be. What could it do? As a radiation weapon it wouldn't have a very wide range – I hope.'

Joe turned towards the door. 'Maybe it's just as well that you broke that tube.'

The pile of components whose places in the assembly still were to be determined was astonishingly small, Cal thought, as he left the lab shortly after midnight.

Many of the circuits were complete and had been tested, with a response that might or might not be adequate for their design. At least nothing blew up.

The following afternoon, Joe called again. 'We've lost

our connection. I just got a TWX from Continental. They want to know what the devil we're talking about in our letter of yesterday – the one asking for a replacement.'

There was only a long silence.

'Cal – you still there?'

'Yes, I'm here. Get hold of Oceanic Tube Company for me. Ask them to send one of their best engineers down here – Jerry Lanier if he's in the plant now. We'll see if they can rebuild the tube for us.'

'That *is* going to cost money.'

'I'll pay it out of my own pocket if I have to. This thing is almost finished.'

Why had they cut their connection, Cal wondered? Had they discovered that their contact had been a mistake? And what would happen if he did finish the interocitor? He wondered if there would be anyone to communicate with even if he did complete it.

It was so close to completion now that he was beginning to suffer from the customary engineer's jitters that come when a harebrained scheme is finally about to be tested. Only this was about a thousand times worse because he didn't even know that he would recognize the correct operation of the interocitor if he saw it.

Jerry Lanier finally showed up. Cal gave him only the broken catherimine tube and allowed him to see none of the rest of the equipment.

Jerry scowled at the tube. 'Since when did they put squirrel cages in glass envelopes? What is this thing?'

'Top hush-hush,' said Cal. 'All I want to know is can you duplicate it?'

'Sure. Where did you get it?'

'Military secret.'

'It looks simple enough. We could probably duplicate it in three weeks or so.'

'Look, Larry, I want that bottle in three days.'

'Cal, you know we can't – '

'Oceanic isn't the only tube maker in the business. This might turn out to be pretty hot stuff.'

'All right, you horse trader. Guarantee it by air express in five days.'

'Good enough.'

For two straight nights Cal didn't go home. He grabbed a half hour's snooze on a lab bench in the early morning. And on the second day he was almost caught by the first lab technician who arrived.

But the interocitor was finished.

The realization seemed more like a dream than reality but every one of the nearly five thousand parts had at last been incorporated into the assembly behind the panels – except the broken tube.

He knew it was right. With a nearly obsessive conviction he felt sure that he had constructed the interocitor just as the unknown engineers had designed it.

He locked the screen room and left word with Joe to call him if Jerry sent the tube, then went home to sleep the clock around.

When he finally went back to the lab a dozen production problems on the airline transmitter had turned up and for once he was thankful for them. They helped reduce the tension of waiting.

He was still working on the job of breaking down one of the transmitter sub-assemblies when quitting time came. It was only because Nell Joy, the receptionist in the front hall, was waiting for her boy friend that he received the package at all.

She called him at twenty after five.

'Mr Meacham? I didn't know whether you'd still be here or not. There's a delivery man here with a package. It looks important. Do you want it tonight?'

'I'll say I do!'

He was out by her desk, signing for the package, almost before she hung up. He tore off the wrappings on the way back to the lab.

4

It was as beautiful a job of duplication as he could have wished for. Cal could have sworn there was no visual difference between it and the original. But the electrical test would tell the story.

In the lab he put the duplicate tube in the tester he'd devised and checked the albion. That was the critical factor.

He frowned as the meter indicated ten percent deviation, but two of the originals had tolerances that great. It would do.

His hand didn't seem quite steady as he put the tube in its socket. He stood back a moment, viewing the completed instrument.

Then he plunged the master switch on the power panel.

He watched anxiously the flickering hands of two-score meters as he advanced along the panels, energizing the circuits one by one.

Intricate adjustments on the panel controls brought the meter readings into line with the catalogue specifications which he had practically memorized by now – but which were written by the meters for safety.

Then slowly, the grayish screen of the cubical viewing tube brightened. Waves of polychrome hue washed over it. It seemed as if an image were trying to form but it remained out of focus, only a wash of color.

'Turn up the intensifier knob,' a masculine voice said suddenly. 'That will clear your screen.'

To Cal it was like words coming suddenly at midnight in a ghost-ridden house. The sound had come out of the utter unknown into which the interocitor reached – but it was human.

He stepped back to the panel and adjusted the knob. The shapeless color flowed into solid lines, congealed to an image. And Cal stared.

He didn't know what he had expected. But the prosaic color-image of the man who watched him from the plate was too ordinary after the weeks-long effort expended on the interocitor.

Yet there was something of the unknown in the man's eyes too – something akin to the unknown of the interocitor. Cal drew slowly nearer the plate, his eyes unable to leave that face, his breath hard and fast.

'Who are you?' he said almost inaudibly. 'What have I built?'

For a moment the man made no answer, as if he hadn't heard. His image was stately, and he appeared of uncertain middle age. He was large and ruggedly attractive of feature. But it was his eyes that held Cal – eyes which seemed to hold an awareness of responsibility to all the people of the world.

'We'd about given you up,' the man said at last. 'But you've passed. And rather well, too.'

'Who are you? What is this – this interocitor I've constructed?'

'The interocitor is simply an instrument of communication. Constructing it was a good deal more.

'I am the employment representative of a group – a certain group who are urgently in need of men, expert technologists. We have a good many stringent requirements for prospective employees. So we require them to take an aptitude test to measure some of those qualifications we desire.

'You have passed that test!'

For a moment Cal stared uncomprehendingly. 'What

do you mean? I have made no application to work with your – your employers.'

A faint trace of a smile crossed the man's face. 'No. No one does that. We pick our own applicants and test them, quite without their awareness that they are being tested. You are to be congratulated on your showing.'

'What makes you think I'd be interested in working for your employers?'

'You would not have come this far unless you were interested in the job we have to offer.'

'I don't understand.'

'You have seen the type of technology in our possession. No matter who or what we are, having come this far you would pursue us to the ends of the Earth to find out how we came by that technology and to learn its mastery for yourself. Is it not so?'

The arrogant truth of the man's statement rocked Cal. There was no uncertainty in the man's voice. He *knew* what Cal was going to do more surely than Cal had known himself up to this moment.

'You seem pretty certain of that.' Cal found it hard to keep an impulsive hostility out of his voice.

'I am. We pick our applicants carefully. We make offers only to those we are certain will accept. Now, since you are about to join us, I will relieve your mind of some unnecessary tensions.

'It has undoubtedly occurred to you, as to all thinking people of your day, that the scientists have done a particularly abominable job of dispensing the tools they have devised. Like careless and indifferent workmen they have tossed the products of their craft to gibbering apes and baboons. The results have been disastrous, to say the least.

'Not all scientists, however, have been quite so indifferent. There are a group of us who have formed an

35

organization for the purpose of obtaining better and more conservative distribution of these tools. We call ourselves, somewhat dramatically perhaps, but none the less truthfully, *Peace Engineers*. Our motives are sure to encompass whatever implications you can honestly make of the term.

'But we need men – technicians, men of imagination, men of good will, men of superb engineering abilities – and our method has to be somewhat less than direct. Hence, our approach to you. It involved simply an interception of mail in a manner you would not yet understand.

'You passed your aptitude test and so were more successful than some of your fellow engineers in this community.'

Cal thought instantly of Edmunds and the toothless gears and the tumbling barrel compound.

'Those other things – ' he said. 'They would have led to the same solution?'

'Yes. In a somewhat different way, of course. But that is all the information I can give you at this time. The next consideration is your coming here.'

'*Where?* Where are you? How do I come?'

The readiness with which his mind accepted the fact of his going shocked him. Was there no other alternative that he should consider? For what reasons should he ally himself with this unknown band who called themselves *Peace Engineers*? He sought for rational reasons why he should not.

There were few that he could muster up. None, actually. He was alone, without family or obligations. He had no particular professional ties to prevent him from leaving.

As for any potential personal threat that might lie in alliance with the *Peace Engineers* – well, he wasn't much afraid of anything that could happen to him personally.

36

But in reality none of these factors had any influence. There was only one thing that concerned him. He had to know more about that fantastic technology they possessed.

And they had known that was the one factor capable of drawing him.

The interviewer paused as if sensing what was in Cal's mind. 'You will learn the answers to all your questions in proper order,' he said. 'Can you be ready tomorrow?'

'I'm ready now,' Cal said.

'Tomorrow will be soon enough. Our plane will land on your airfield at six P.M. It will remain fifteen minutes. It will take off without you if you are not in it by that time. You will know it by its color. A black ship with a single horizontal orange stripe.

'That is all. Congratulations and good luck to you. I'll be looking forward to seeing you personally.

'Stand back, now. When I cut off, the interocitor will be destroyed. Stand back!'

Cal backed sharply to the far side of the room. He saw the man's head nod, his face smiling a pleasant good-bye, then the image vanished from the screen.

Almost instantly there came the hiss of burning insulation, the crack of heat-shattered glass. From the framework of the interocitor rose a blooming bubble of smoke that slowly filled the room as wires melted and insulation became molten and ran.

Cal burst from the screen room and grasped a nearby fire extinguisher, which he played into the blinding smoke pouring from the room. He emptied that one and ran for another.

Slowly the heat and smoke dispelled. He moved back into the room and knew that the interocitor could never be analyzed or duplicated from that ruin. Its destruction had been complete.

It was useless trying to sleep that night. He sat in the park until after midnight, when a suspicious cop chased him off. After that he simply walked the streets until dawn, trying to fathom the implications of what he'd seen and heard.

Peace Engineers –

What did the term mean? It could imply a thousand things, a secret group with dictatorial ambitions in possession of a powerful technology – a bunch of crackpots with strange access to genius – or it could be what the term literally implied.

But there was no guarantee that their purposes were altruistic. With his past knowledge of human nature he was more inclined to credit the possibility that he was being led into some Sax Rohmer melodrama.

At dawn he turned towards his apartment. He finally slept a while and cleaned up and ate and left the rent and a note instructing the landlord regarding his belongings. He went to the plant in the midafternoon and resigned amidst a storm of protests from Billingsworth and a forty-percent salary increase offer.

That done, it was nearly evening and he went up to see Joe Wilson.

'I wondered what happened to you this morning,' said Joe. 'I tried to call you for a couple of hours.'

'I slept late,' said Cal. 'I just came in to resign.'

'Resign?' Joe Wilson stared incredulously. 'What for? What about the interocitor?'

'It blew up in my face. The whole thing's gone.'

'I hoped you would make it,' Joe said a little sadly. 'I wonder if we will ever find out where that stuff came from.'

'Sure,' said Cal carelessly. 'It was just some shipping mixup. We'll find out about it someday.'

'Cal – ' Joe Wilson was looking directly into his face. 'You found out, didn't you?'

Cal hesitated a moment. He had been put under no bond of secrecy. What could it matter? He understood something of the fascination the problem held for a frustrated engineer turned into a technical purchasing agent.

'Yes,' he said. 'I found out.'

Joe smiled wryly. 'I was hoping you would. Can you tell me about it?'

'There's nothing to tell. I don't know where they are. All I know is that I talked to someone. They offered me a job.'

They waited together until at last he saw it coming in low and fast, a black and orange ship. Wing flaps down, it slowed and touched the runway. Already it was like the symbol of a vast and important future that had swept him up. Already the familiar surroundings of Ryberg's were something out of a dim and unimportant past.

'I wish we could have learned more about the interocitor,' said Joe.

Cal's eyes were still straining towards the ship as it taxied around on the field. Then he shook hands solemnly with Joe. 'You and me both,' he said. 'Believe me – '

Joe Wilson stood by the window and, as Cal went out towards the ship, he knew he'd been correct in that glimpse he'd got of the cockpit canopy silhouetted against the sky.

The ship was pilotless.

Another whispering clue to a mighty, alien technology.

He knew Cal must have seen it, too, but Cal's steps were steady as he walked towards it.

5

He must have slept during part of that fantastic night flight. He could remember only the incessant thunder of the engine in front of him and the starlit sky of night above. He remembered the tumultuous flashes of lightning as the ship skirted a vast thunder storm.

Now daylight was racing him out of the east, lighting the cirrus miles above him and shading the desert below. Still the ghostly ship gave no sign of slowing its determined flight.

His hands and feet searched with involuntary constancy for the absent controls. It gave him a sense of helpless imprisonment when he considered that utterly blank cockpit in which he rode. Not a control, not a single instrument – only the thunder of the motor and the propeller and the shriek of the air.

He looked over the edge at the brightening landscape below. About eight thousand feet up, he thought. He strained to recognize familiarity in the terrain below. It looked like cattle country. Oklahoma, Texas, New Mexico or Arizona, perhaps. Distant cliffs of shining vermilion made him fairly certain that it was a Southwest region, probably in one of the latter two states.

While the sun overtook him, Cal watched the passage of tiny towns, the puff of occasional whirlwinds on the desert, the creeping cars that sometimes appeared on a distant highway.

Then, suddenly, the plane dipped. Cal reached for the absent stick, listened critically to the thunder of the motor. Twisting around, he glanced at the elevators. They were depressed to lose altitude.

He scanned the horizon ahead and the vast empty land below. Fat humps of mountains projected from the desert. Then he saw in the distance the haze that hovered over some desert city. The ship seemed to be heading for it.

He did not know this country. As the plane approached the town he saw that he was not headed directly for it but was going north towards a small valley that lay on the other side of low humped mountains.

In the valley were a cluster of buildings. Several hundred houses surrounded a plant composed of four long blank-walled structures and a fifth, much larger, that was in the process of construction.

The plane soared over the plant and circled twice. A small landing field was just west of the four buildings. There was a hangar with a sock hanging limp in the windless air. Nearby was a small building that crouched beneath a giant antenna, a great bowl-like screen that turned slowly on gimbals, ever pointing – straight toward the little plane in which he rode.

The control, he thought – All through those dark hours this mass of metal had been the mysterious beacon that guided the plane.

There were a half-dozen men watching the ship from the field but not with any apparent curiosity. They had the appearance of waiting for a routine flight to be completed.

Dust spurted from the earth as the wheels touched. Cal watched the flaps go down and sensed the dragging hand that slowed the ship. It taxied up to the apron before the hangar. The motor died and grunted to a stop in the shadow of the great bowl of the guiding antenna.

It was like the end of a dream in which a sense of sleep

still prevails over the senses. He saw the men approaching, saw their mouths move in greeting, but he made no move to stir. One of the mechanics climbed to the wing step and shoved the canopy back. The fresh coolness of the morning desert air brushed his face.

'Did you have a good trip, sir?' The mechanic was smiling. Just a kid in white overalls, he didn't seem awed by the landing of a ship without controls.

Cal nodded. 'No complaint about the trip. But I would like to know where this is.'

'That was Phoenix, Arizona, you saw coming in. We're just north of town.'

Cal grunted as he rose stiffly and climbed out. 'That's something. I was afraid I was going to end up on Calabuluska Island where the meemies eat the white people.'

'I don't blame you for getting the willies out of a ride like that. I don't want any of it myself. The beam is used mainly for a lot of other things but I guess the Engineer figured he might as well use it to pick up new employees as well.'

'The Engineer?'

'The boss of the whole place. I've never even seen him myself. His name is Jorkovnosnitch or something like that, and he doesn't call himself president, just Engineer. So that's what everybody else calls him too, because they forget how to pronounce his name.'

His knees buckled a trifle as Cal jumped from the wing to the ground. He stood a moment to steady himself and looked over the landscape. The people looked human. The plant looked like a lot of other medium sized industrial plants set out near some small city for decentralization purposes.

But the plane behind him, that towering beam director that was now stilled – these belied the appearance of normalcy. These and a director who called himself simply the Engineer and manufactured devices employing a completely strange technology –

There was a stir. Eyes were suddenly directed a short distance down the field. A slim, dark-haired girl was approaching. She wore a white tailored suit whose severity was relieved by the gentle fluffing of her hair as she walked swiftly towards them.

She held out a hand towards Cal as she came up. 'I'm Dr Adams – Ruth Adams,' she added as if to invite a more friendly level of acquaintance than the stiff 'Dr' would imply.

'I'm Cal Meacham,' he said, 'but I suppose you know that – '

He stopped awkwardly. The girl's hand felt icy cold. It was firm and competent but – almost imperceptibly – it trembled.

He glanced down. She withdrew it quickly and smiled. 'I know quite a bit about you. I'm assistant in the employment department and your files were referred to me for analysis. My doctorate is in psychiatry.'

'Yes – yes,' he said absently. He was watching her face, narrowing his field of vision to block out the gentle lips, the firm molded cheeks, tinted softly with desert tan – narrowing to her eyes. They were big and soft brown in tone.

And the utter fear that dwelt in them was like an electric shock through his body.

Only when he concentrated on her eyes did he get that intense message of fear she could not hide. But she was so constantly animated that he could not long hold to such a narrow field of vision.

He attempted a smile to break the awkward pause he had created. 'This seems to be purely a routine affair to the boys here but it's quite a jolt for me. I'd like to know what this is all about. I spoke to a man over a device

43

called an interocitor. I didn't learn his name but he offered me a job and I took him up on it. He sent this pilotless plane for me and here I am.'

'Yes, that was Dr Warner who spoke with you,' said Ruth. Cal found it impossible to think of her as Dr Adams.

'I work under him,' she continued. 'He selects all engineers. He was so pleased by your aptitudes and your work that he sent me out personally to bring you to him. Ordinary employees rate only an office boy.'

She assumed an attitude of mock regality and they burst out laughing together. Cal almost forgot the fear he had seen in her eyes.

'I appreciate the special attention,' he said. 'A freckle-faced office boy certainly would have spoiled my day.'

'Come with me. I'll take you to Dr Warner now.'

He took her arm lightly as she led the way over the dust-covered apron of the hangar towards the nearest of the four plant buildings. Even in that bright sunlight he felt a faint tremor in her body – as if with cold.

Dr Warner looked much as he had on the screen of the interocitor tube. A few sparse strands of white hair still adhered to the middle of his pate. A gently protruding paunch was beginning to tell the effects of years at a desk. Yet his face had the tinge of a man used to days out of doors.

He advanced with outstretched hand as soon as Ruth Adams entered his office with Cal in tow. 'Mr Meacham!' He pumped Cal's hand vigorously. 'Please sit down. You too, Ruth.

'You want to know all about us, of course,' said Dr Warner. 'You want to know our purposes, our means of operation, who we are, why we are, what we intend to do, what we expect of you and in general where you go from here.'

'I guess that would just about cover it,' said Cal. 'You've been asked those questions before.'

'Many times. And all of them can be answered in good time. I think you can realize, however, that your initial period here will be in the nature of a probation. The answers to your questions will be given gradually. I'm sure that's reasonable.'

'Of course.'

'I told you that we believe the world could better utilize the productions of science if scientists themselves placed some restrictions on the use of their talents. In effect, we are on strike against destructive uses. We propose to control the products of our research from here on.

'Already, we have uncovered principles and invented devices that the military cliques of the world would give their eyes for, provided they knew we had them.'

'But how can such principles be utilized without being revealed to the military?'

'Some can't. Those are suppressed. Others are released with such controls as will insure their proper use. The interocitor is an example of this.'

'How?'

'It is a superb communication device, surpassing common radio principles in a thousand ways. But it can be instantly blanked out or totally destroyed – as you witnessed – the moment it is used for communicating lying propaganda or anything else harmful to the mind of man.'

'You consider yourselves censors of all that man does!'

'No – merely of the uses to which our inventions are put. That right of censorship is inherent in the invention or discovery, we submit. Until now it has never been enforced.'

'That's a pretty big order.'

Warner smiled. 'Sometimes we think we are pretty big men. At least we operate on that principle with the silent hope that we just don't get too big for our pants. Somebody had to make the attempt. We are doing it – and rather successfully so far. The militarists would be appalled if they knew the brain power that we have succeeded in draining away from their projects. Including yours – '

'I don't think they will miss me much. I was already – on strike, as you say.'

'That's what I mean. So were thousands of others. We are men who are not interested in science for the sake of "pure" science, whatever that is. We are interested in science as a tool in man's rise from the ape to whatever goal may be possible when his vast potentialities are fully realized. Those who have not come very far from the ape are using that tool with destructive effects which must be curbed. That sums our entire purpose. You are in agreement, of course.'

Cal Meacham nodded slowly. 'And doubtful of any man's ability to achieve such a purpose – at least in our day.'

'We shall try to convince you as we proceed,' said Dr Warner. 'But now for your duties here. You have seen the plant under construction. That is nearly completed and is to be an interocitor assembly plant. We want to assign you in charge of that plant.'

Cal stared as if he hadn't heard correctly. 'In charge – of that plant!'

'Yes. That is correct.'

'But I'm just a lab punk. I was only a project engineer at Ryberg. I haven't had a background for that sort of thing.'

'We've investigated your background thoroughly. We

are satisfied with your qualifications. You will receive an intensive training by the design engineers who produced the interocitor and by the production men now handling it. You will be amply prepared for the job. You will take it, of course.'

Cal smiled. 'I wish you would put a question mark at the end of one of those statements about me. I get the uncomfortable feeling you know too much about me.'

'Not too much – enough. We have to. And that is about all I can tell you at the moment. You will learn other details of our operations as you go along. Eventually, you will meet Mr Jorgasnovara, Engineer of the entire project, but it may be months. He's an elusive man.

'Dr Adams will introduce you to the surroundings and your fellow engineers and give you directions in beginning the training which will be necessary. I need not remind you, of course, that your being in charge of interocitor assembly is only a first step in your progress here, but it is an important step.'

Warner rose and extended a hand. 'It's been a great pleasure to know you. I'll be constantly available for any questions or problems that arise.'

6

It was almost a letdown – the contrast between his strange
introduction to the Engineers via the interocitor and this
seemingly prosaic industrial plant here in the desert.
Nothing out of the ordinary seemed to be going on here –
nothing, that is, except the manufacture of the interocitor.
And a girl whose eyes were haunted with a fear she could
not always hide.

She spent the remainder of the morning with him. He
learned that her psychiatric work in the employment
department was highly essential in testing, judging and
training the peculiarly unique individuals required for
work in the plant.

They went on a tour of the plant. Two of the buildings,
he found, were devoted entirely to development engineering. Over five hundred engineers were employed in scores
of projects.

Everything that a researcher could desire was at their
disposal. The prodigality of equipment almost made him
weak when he thought of the penny-pinching controls
imposed at Ryberg, where he'd had to fight tooth and nail
for every hundred dollars a project cost.

This was an engineer's paradise!

Ruth Adams sensed what was in his mind as he looked
over the beautifully equipped laboratories. 'You'll enjoy
working here. Anything these men want is theirs for the
whistling.'

'But it costs heavy money for equipment like this!'

'The company is quite profitable. The Engineer and
other heads are not just visionaries.'

48

She introduced him to many of the engineers and section directors. He was not surprised to find a number of professional acquaintances and personal friends among them.

Among them was Ole Swenberg, a big blond fellow he had known very well at college. He had often wondered what had happened to Ole. They had not met since the war.

Ole beamed and ran across the lab to grasp Cal's hand when he recognized him.

'By golly, Cal, I thought it was about time you were showing up here. The way you used to talk when we were in school I expected to find you running the place.'

'I hid out. What are you doing here, you big Swede?'

'Any darned thing I please and that's the truth. I don't have to worry about publishing a paper every three weeks in some stinking journal – "for the prestige of the department" – either. I stayed on at college and taught four years before I got fed up. What are you geared up for?'

'They tell me I'm going to direct the interocitor assembly for a while.'

'Boy, have *you* got yourself a job! That's hot stuff. They tried to farm it out and no plant in the country could handle it. That's why you've got it. But it's lunch time. Come on. It's on me.'

They followed the garrulous Ole to the plant cafeteria, and listened to the account of how he was revolutionizing the world of science with his discoveries – with the small help of the group of Peace Engineers as a whole. But lunch time was not long enough for him to finish.

'Tell you what,' he said, as they finished. 'How about a small beer bust in your diggings tonight? You haven't told me a thing about what you've been doing. Ruth and I'll come over and give you the real lowdown on what you're in for. That okay with you, Ruth?'

She smiled tolerantly towards Cal. 'The Swede seems to have it all arranged.'

'Well, that's fine. Only I don't have any diggings exactly,' said Cal. 'What do I do in that case?'

'Oh, you have one of the company houses available unless you prefer something in town. It's more convenient out here,' said Ruth.

'Suits me.'

Cal spent the afternoon unpacking and getting settled in his quarters. He had two comfortable rooms and a kitchenette in case he wanted to do any cooking, but he expected to take his meals at the cafeteria.

Finished with stowing his gear, he sank down on the sofa and looked out the window towards the strange plant where unheard-of technology produced gadgets called interocitors.

It was a weird set-up in some ways, but for the first time in his life he felt completely at ease in his place of work. In the industrial plants he'd known, engineers were constantly shifting from one place to another, moving around, looking for offers, eternally trying to 'get somewhere.'

None of them could ever define that mystic goal, but they knew the same common sense of deep frustration. They battled each other, trying to make their company's product cheaper, trying to make their electric razor or toaster or radio a bit better than their fellow engineers who worked for other concerns. But, like paid gladiators, they felt no loyalty except that which was inspired by their paychecks.

He had run in that professional rat race for many years. After college he worked for Acme Electric, then he found a better offer at Midwest. Corning had offered a little more money. He had found better working conditions at

Colonial. Then Ryberg had seemed to be a better research set-up –

It would have gone on the rest of his life. He'd have landed a department directorship somewhere. Maybe he'd have married. After fifty years they would have given him a gold watch.

It was over. The Engineers were no gold watch outfit. It was too good to be true – too good to last.

Ole and Ruth knocked on his door at eight. Ole had a half dozen brown bottles in his hand and Ruth had a basket of sandwiches.

'We knew you'd be hungry,' she said. 'You don't look like the cooking type of bachelor.'

'Believe me, I'm not.'

'See what I told you,' said Ole loudly to Ruth. 'This is a chance you can't afford to miss.'

'Oh, for heaven's sake, Ole!'

Cal smiled and looked from one to the other. He wondered how a serene person like Ruth Adams happened to be going around with the loud-mouthed Ole.

They sat down and Ole became suddenly serious. 'We didn't come for just a social call, Cal.'

'What, then? I thought you liked my company. Is this place business twenty-four hours a day?'

'Our kind of business is. What kind of an aptitude test did they give you?'

'The interocitor. They teased me into building one from a catalogue.'

'Know what mine was? A book that made a page-at-a-glance reader out of me. I ordered some new texts from a company and these things came. I looked at a page – and it stuck. Nothing on it ever left me. Couldn't get rid of it if I wanted to. The most intricate circuit diagrams you can imagine. One glance and they're mine. Pretty neat, eh?'

'Sounds wonderful. I'd like to see some.'

'You will. They're used in parts of the training you'll get. You'll get a brainful of stuff you never dreamed was in heaven or earth.

'When I first got those books I tore them apart molecule by molecule to find out what made them tick. I never did find out but I became a biologist, and biochemist as well as an electronics engineer in the process. The Engineers liked my attack, even if it was a failure, so they took me on.'

'Do they have a different test for everyone?'

'No. You're the first one, however, that I've known who got the interocitor. That's been top hush-hush stuff. They needed you pretty badly.'

'I'd like to know more about how these Peace Engineers operate. I suppose I'll get the dope in time as Warner says, but I wish you could tell me a little more.'

Ole looked bleak. 'Cal, do you believe that guff?'

'What do you mean, guff?'

'About the Peace Engineers. All this phony window dressing.'

Cal sat up straight on the edge of his seat. He felt as if someone had dealt him a blow underneath his ribs. 'What are you talking about? You mean this thing isn't on the level?'

'Ole –' Ruth interrupted. 'Let me talk.'

'Sure. You can make it sound more reasonable.'

'When I first came here,' she said, 'I was appalled by the naïveté of the scientists and engineers who make the wonderful machines of which our civilization boasts.

'Peace Engineers! They knew that half the scientists of the country were sick at heart after the last war because of what had happened through the discoveries of science. It was the most obvious bait they could hold out. And the best brains in the nation bit on it.'

'Who are "they"?'

52

'That's what we don't know. Ole and I and a dozen or so others of the engineers have become – to put it mildly – suspicious of the whole set-up. And our suspicions have frightened us.

'There is absolutely no organization, no society or fraternal group called "Peace Engineers" as you might expect. There is nothing but this plant and a group of engineers who work here just as in any other industrial plant – that and the incredible technology that someone possesses. After all the talk about Peace Engineers there is still nothing but – a vacuum.

'Technology in a vacuum. An incredibly advanced technology. You know more about it than either of us do. Under what kind of circumstances would it be produced?'

'Time and money – great quantities of both would be required. But I supposed they had both.'

'Ruth has missed an important point,' said Ole. 'It's more than technology. There's new basic science involved. Science that speaks of a culture almost wholly foreign to anything we know about.'

'I'm inclined to agree with that,' said Cal thoughtfully. 'But does that prohibit the Peace Engineers from originating it, and if so, where did it come from?'

'That's what scares us. Look at what's happening – the cream of the scientific brains of the nation are working for the Engineers. Suppose they aren't so peaceful in spite of their name? Suppose that it is really an enormous camouflage for war preparation? Suppose they are giving us minor secrets in return for the privilege of milking our scientific genius for all they can.'

'There are two things wrong with those arguments. You just got through pointing out that these things are not exactly minor. By comparison, we aren't contributing very much for what we get.'

'Don't kid yourself. Our best brains being applied to

this advanced basic science are producing plenty. And suppose that what we have seen is relatively minor compared with what we haven't seen?'

Cal leaned back heavily. 'I can't speak from experience yet but I think you're on the wrong track. An enemy could hardly operate like this under the nose of our own military.'

'Who said anything about enemy?' said Ole. 'Isn't it just as bad in the long run if our own military has corralled these brains by this deception? In fact, that seems to be the more likely explanation.'

'We're not arguing for any one conclusion,' said Ruth abruptly. 'We don't *know*. We're simply saying that this whole front of Peace Engineer propaganda is false. We want to know what's back of it. It scares us to think what might lie behind this secretly controlled technology.

'But we can't go to any authorities and tell them we're scared and ask them to investigate the place. There is absolutely nothing we can do unless we find out who is behind the Peace Engineers.'

'That's where we need your help,' said Ole. 'You're going to be in a high and responsible place around here. If anyone is in a position to get behind this false front you ought to be able to. Will you help us find out what is going on here?'

'No,' said Cal. 'The one thing I've looked for all my life is here! I'm willing to grant whoever originated this technology some rights to secrecy regarding the dispersal of it. I'm going to play ball with them until I find out differently and it will take a lot more than these suspicions of yours to change my mind!'

'You don't have to get sore,' said Ole. '*Just try to find out.* You'll get curious sooner or later. Then you'll beat your head against the stone wall just like the rest of us are beginning to do. And then maybe you'll begin to get scared, too, when you realize that no one here knows a thing about whose hand is behind all this.'

He wasn't sore, Cal thought, as he lay in the darkness vainly trying to sleep long after their departure. He wasn't sore, but he was more than irritated by their jumping him with their suspicions on his first night here.

Certainly, in every organization there were soreheads who didn't like the way things went. He would never have suspected Ole or Ruth of being such, however. But he could scarcely be more generous after what he had heard from them.

And yet – that wasn't the whole story and he knew it. The fear he had seen in those dark eyes of Ruth was a real and tangible thing to her. It was no mere fantasy.

But he would wait. In one respect they were right. In his position he might have opportunity to study the organization as a whole. When he found the answers to their questions he could put their minds at ease. He felt certain the answers would not be what they suspected.

7

For the next six months his days and nights were spent in the most intensive study he had ever done. The engineering specifications and basic physical principles behind the interocitor were thrown open to him. He pored over the books. He built up components, tore them down again – until he was certain he could build an interocitor blindfolded and with one hand tied behind his back.

In all that time he did not once meet the Engineer, Jorgasnovara, although the man was pointed out to him. Warner had promised that he would be introduced and Cal wondered when the time would come.

It was a wonderful day when he at last saw the assembly lines in full operation and tested the first completed equipment as it came off the line. He had gained skill in executive leadership and he had a smoothly running plant that required only top direction of the most general kind.

It gave him a breathing spell, a measure of freedom to contemplate the significance of what he had accomplished, freedom to review his position, freedom to question –

During those busy months he had found little time to talk to Ruth. At first she'd been his guide in getting him acquainted at the plant, but gradually his entire time had been taken up with other engineers. It had been five weeks, he thought suddenly, since he had even seen her.

He reached for the phone and called her extension.

Her voice was a pleasant sound in his ear. 'Ruth! I thought you would be over for the christening. The lines are moving.'

'Hello, Cal. I heard about it but I was too busy to get over. Dr Warner is very pleased with your success, and the Engineer thinks highly of your work. In fact, I was to call you and let you know that he's coming in and wants to talk with you, probably tomorrow.'

'Well, how about a little delayed celebration?'

'Such as what?'

'Oh, nothing fancy. A dinner in town, maybe. Then just go for a ride.'

For a moment there was no sound from the receiver, then she said hesitantly, 'All right, Cal. I'd love to. Pick me up at my place. I live in town, you know.'

As he scribbled her address after hanging up he reflected that he hadn't known. He hadn't learned a thing about her in all the time he'd been here. He didn't know where Ole fitted in, but that didn't worry him much. Ole was a good guy but he wasn't for Ruth.

And Cal found himself wondering again about those fears of Ruth. He had found nothing to substantiate them, yet he couldn't forget her eyes as they had looked that first day.

He picked her up at eight. She was dressed in a soft gray evening dress and wore the tiny orchid he had sent. It was utterly impossible to think of an MD and PhD in that dress. He didn't try.

There was no hint of distress in her. She was pleasant and gay at dinner and not once did the talk go back to their work at the plant or her feelings about the place.

Afterward he headed the car beyond the outskirts of town. They stopped with the radio on to watch the moon-washed desert.

But her mood seemed to have changed once they left the lights of the restaurant. She settled in silence in the far corner of the seat. A panicky thought occurred to him that he might have offended by stopping. He moved to start the car again.

'Oh, don't, Cal – let's watch it for a while.'

'I thought – ' he fumbled.

'I got a letter from Ole the other day,' said Ruth abruptly.

'Letter? Where is he? I haven't seen him for a couple of months but I thought he was still around the plant.'

'No, he's gone.' She was looking straight ahead, her voice ending each flat statement with finality as if not willing to volunteer more.

'Why? Where did he go? Was it – what you tried to tell me about – that night six months ago?'

She nodded slowly. 'Ole found out. I wanted you to see him and talk to him. Maybe you could have understood what he was trying to say. I made an attempt to call you but you weren't there. And then they came for Ole and took him away. They wouldn't let me see him again – until they had changed him.'

'Changed him? What are you talking about, Ruth? Did they do something to Ole?'

She turned slightly towards him so that he could see the moonlight full on her face. It lent a ghostly radiance and heightened the returning fear in her eyes.

'He broke down with hysteria in his lab one day,' she said. 'His assistants brought him to me. He kept babbling about some fearful thing he'd seen in the sky but I couldn't understand it. And then for just a moment he grew more coherent and said that he'd been working on some interocitor modifications and suddenly he'd heard the Engineer thinking.'

'*Thinking!*'

'That's the word he used. He was in such a state of violent terror that I should have given him a quieting hypo immediately, but that was when I tried to get you. I thought maybe you would understand. And then they came and took him away.'

'Who?'

'Warner and a couple of his medical assistants. They said they would be able to take care of him, but they wouldn't let me come along. Afraid he'd get too violent, they said.'

'What happened?'

'Nothing. I saw Ole the next day. He acted as if very little had occurred. He refused to talk in detail about what had happened and told me he was leaving. That was all he would say.'

'Why didn't you tell me this before?'

'I don't know. I thought perhaps I could get more out of Ole later so that I would have proof for you – but I couldn't. I guess I shouldn't have told you tonight except that now that Ole's gone I can't talk to anyone about what I think. The others seem to be too absorbed in their wonderful laboratory privileges to criticize. They're closing their eyes to the suspicions they had.'

She turned suddenly and looked into his eyes. 'Cal, won't you go and see Ole and try to find out what he learned?'

Cal remained silent. What could they have done to Ole, he wondered. Did they have a method of taking care of disgruntled employees to keep them from talking? Some method that was on a par with the rest of this advanced technology? That would explain how their secret could be so well kept without benefit of military suppression.

'I think I'd like to see Ole,' he said. 'I wish you had told me this before. Isn't it possible they just sent him away to keep him from disturbing the morale of others with his suspicions?'

'I don't doubt that they did! But that doesn't explain what happened to Ole to make him so deathly frightened.'

'Maybe they arranged that, too.'

'I could believe that. But what about the interocitor? I don't know anything about the physical science involved in it – but can you honestly say you know *everything* about the device? Ole didn't think so and it was when he was experimenting on it that he had his fit of hysteria.'

'Look – nobody can say he knows *everything* about even an ordinary radio set.'

'You know what I mean. A radio has a known function and will perform that function when it is properly operating. But are you absolutely certain you know all the proper functions of an interocitor?'

'Well – yeah, sure – hang it all, Ruth, the jigger is so infernally complicated that even while I think I know all about it I still can't say that it might not be capable of something I don't know about. But why should I suspect it?'

'Because the Peace Engineers set-up is a phony.'

'That brings us around in a complete circle.'

'You forget what happened to Ole. If I'm right – and you don't believe me – I'm putting my life in your hands by telling you this. I'm sure of that.'

He reached out and drew her into the curve of his arm. He could feel the tension of her body as he had that first day they met.

'Ruth, you're exaggerating! I'm not saying I won't believe you. Perhaps you are right – engineers are simple-minded folk who can be fooled by almost any kind of make-believe. Armies would still fight with swords and slings if it weren't so.

'On the other hand, because this place is so close to the engineering paradise I've always dreamed about I don't want to get kicked out for going around asking the top guys if they've signed loyalty pledges.'

'You're laughing at me,' she said bitterly.

'I'm not. I promise I'll do everything I can to find out if you and Ole are right. He was my friend. You shouldn't have kept me from knowing what had happened to him.'

'I'm sorry. I didn't think you'd care much, really.'

'I'll keep my mouth shut around the plant, but I'll let you know everything I find out.'

'Tomorrow you'll see the Engineer,' she said prophetically. 'Then you'll know.'

He had once glimpsed the Engineer from a distance as the plant director climbed into his personal plane on the landing field. From that one glimpse he knew the man was *big*.

Beyond mere physical size, however, there was a *sense* of bigness. This was the first impression that Cal Meacham felt when he stood before the Engineer's desk.

'Sit down.' He motioned to Cal.

'I'm Mr Jorgasnovara,' said the man, smiling slowly. 'I suppose you can see at once why I'm simply referred to as "The Engineer." I rather like the title myself – a vanity, no doubt, but engineering has always seemed about the most important thing in the world to me.'

'I can understand that,' said Cal. He had almost forgotten Ruth's fears and found himself liking the man. Jorgasnovara appeared to be about sixty. His head had scarcely a speck of fuzz to suggest it had ever grown hair. It was large, a high domed cranium, with deep eyes. His cheek bones were wide, sloping just a little to a square jaw.

'I hope you don't think my actions eccentric in that I haven't asked to meet you until now,' he said. 'I have been very well satisfied with your progress and have been content to let you proceed at your own pace while I attended to other details of our plants that were not going so smoothly.'

'Thanks,' said Cal. 'The basic science is still pretty far

61

ahead of me but I feel I'm creeping up on it. It still seems rather incredible that such advances as I see can be accounted for by the time you've had available.'

The Engineer glanced up sharply from the paperweight on his desk. 'How much time do you suppose it has taken?'

'Why, I gathered that you'd just come into existence as an organization since the last war.'

He shook his head. 'This has been a long time in the making – a long time. The technology you see is largely the work of men long dead. Would it surprise you to know that the history of this society goes back to the seventeenth century?'

'That far!'

'A Frenchman – one Jules de Rande – was the first, as far as we know, to conceive the idea. He published his philosophy for the benefit of a few friends in which he proposed that men of talent determine the use to be made of their genius.

'All about him he saw men given patronage, being bought for their intellects and used like articles of war or commerce. He had the brilliance to glimpse the distant future of our own day in which men of science could be bought like ancient mercenaries.

'De Rande succeeded in persuading many of the learned men of his day to hold back. When he died, his philosophy remained in the minds of a few. Sometimes it all but disappeared, then revived in relatively large groups. But always there was a growing mass of scientific knowledge being withheld from the world in the archives of this group.

'Then, during the American Civil War, the Peace Engineers were organized as a definite society. Their work has been continuous and growing since that time.'

'It's almost unbelievable,' said Cal. 'To think that such

a society could exist underground all those years! Were they always ahead of the rest of civilization?'

The Engineer nodded. 'Tungsten lamps were available fifteen years before poor Tom Edison began his first carbon filaments. We knew the principles of high-tension power transmission and could have built electric generators as good as any today.'

The Engineer nodded. 'Tungsten lamps were available fifteen years before poor Tom Edison began his first carbon filaments. We knew the principles of high-tension power transmission and could have built electric generators as good as any today.'

'But withholding all that technology from civilization – '

'Kept the atomic bomb from being used in the First World War instead of the Second. If it had not been so, the Second would perhaps have been the last, and you and I would even now be cowering in caves, snarling over a piece of rotten meat – provided we were alive at all. It was worth it.'

Cal sat back weakly in his chair. Slowly he began to perceive the vast panorama of hidden dreams that lay behind the Peace Engineers –

How wrong Ruth and Ole had been in their suspicions!

'What about those who come into the organization and leave? How has the secret been kept? I am thinking of my old friend, Ole Swenberg.'

'Ole never knew what I have just told you. Neither do any of the others who leave – and there are many who do. They say little about us because they have little to say. Most of them do not even know as much as you did when they first come here.

'We hire them simply as engineers and advance them as their understanding and personalities develop. I may tell you that there is much yet that I have not revealed –

but I have no fear in telling you as much as I have. You will not leave us.'

The certainty in the Engineer's voice sent an odd chill through Cal. 'How can you be so sure of that?'

The Engineer's smile was enigmatic. 'We are quite certain. We know you very well, Mr Meacham.'

The big man seemed to become lost in thought for a moment. The massive lines of his face seemed to slowly shift and form an immobile cast of bleak severity and unknown depth. Cal felt as if he were in the presence of an intellect that had seen the vast stretch of eons of time and light years of space.

Abruptly the man shifted and arose. He extended a massive hand to Cal. 'It's been a pleasure talking with you. There is little more that I have for you at this time. Your work is excellent. I shall see you again from time to time and shortly I think we shall have a new assignment for you.'

8

Cal returned to his own personal laboratory that opened from the executive offices of the interocitor plant. He closed the door and perched on a high lab stool and stared out the windows overlooking the plant buildings.

His feelings churned with doubt and questions he knew not whom to ask. Jorgasnovara's revelation opened up unlimited new channels of speculation. He had no doubt of the truth of the story. What troubled him was the implication behind the admittedly untold portion of the tale.

The factor that seemed most obviously missing to him was a sense of fraternalism, of organization, a missionary-like zeal to obtain their goal. Perhaps in three hundred years such attitudes of the zealot would normally have been replaced with more practical considerations.

But everything he had heard still left unexplained the resignation of Ole Swenberg. As he thought back Cal had to admit that the Engineer had side-stepped quite completely the direct question of just what had happened to Ole. He couldn't help feeling that it had been deliberate.

At the heart of it all lay the mysterious apparatus, the interocitor. What had Ole learned from it? What had he meant by saying he heard the Engineer thinking? Or had Ruth merely misunderstood him in his incoherence?

Cal moved slowly from the stool to the opposite side of the room, where one of the machines stood. He knew how it was built. He understood the gross electrical characteristics of all its components. He knew that it depended upon a mode of transmission that was not electromagnetic radiation.

It was here that his knowledge broke down. In the intensity of his study to learn how the thing could be produced on an assembly line he had not had the time to burrow into the depths of the mathematical theory on which it was based. That, too, was something wholly beyond conventional technology. An entire new mathematical system had to be absorbed in learning that theory.

Perhaps Ruth was right. He still didn't know *all* the functions of the interocitor.

A sudden knock on the door roused him. He opened it, admitting Ruth.

'You saw him?' she said.

'We had quite a little chat.'

'What do you think?'

'That's a hard question to answer. It has to have so many qualifications. I'll admit he is a strange egg, but he's on the level. As far as he's gone he's not attempting to deceive anyone. I'm sure of that.'

'So he won you over that easily.'

'Wait a minute. I said there were qualifications. The big factor lies in what he admits he isn't telling, but I honestly can't see any reason for getting the jitters over it.'

'Ole did.'

'I know. That's what I've been thinking about. I can't understand what he meant when – and if – he said he heard the Engineer thinking – '

'Perhaps he meant just what he said.'

'That this thing can pick up thought waves?' Cal rubbed his chin in the cup of his hand. 'I should have learned better than to say a thing is impossible around here, but I don't see how. And if so, you'd think Jorgasnovara would protect himself against it.'

'Maybe he doesn't know it.'

'I'd hate to bet on that. I'm afraid there isn't much that he doesn't know about what goes on around here.'

'Well, I hope you find out. I – came in to say good-bye, Cal. I'm leaving too. I can't take it any longer, and I don't want to wait until I get the treatment they gave Ole.'

'Leaving! No – wait, Ruth. That's not necessary.'

'I suppose a psychiatrist should know enough about his own emotions to be able to keep from giving way to the jitters but I just can't any longer. The place is oppressive.

'There's something going on that we don't know anything about. Whatever it is, Ole found out, and it nearly scared him out of his mind. I'd hoped that maybe you could find out, but you've been taken in, just like the rest.'

'Look, Ruth – give me a week or a month or whatever it takes. I want to know what happened to Ole just as badly as you do. I promise you that if this interocitor can do any tricks I don't know about I'll find it out.'

She hesitated, her brown eyes peering deeply into his. 'All right,' she agreed. 'I'll wait, but there's one more thing I'd like to know. Do you know what is happening to the interocitors you are making, and where they are being sold?'

He laughed. 'I've been so doggone busy getting the things off the production line that I haven't worried much about that. I leave it up to the sales and shipping department to get rid of them.'

'I went through the shipping department yesterday,' she said. 'There were six hundred units crated for shipment. They were gone this morning.'

'That's our normal production.'

'How did they go out?'

'Truck. They tell me the lines generally pick them up after dark on night runs.'

'Isn't that a bit unusual?'

'I hadn't thought much about it. What difference does it make anyway?'

'It rained last night. There might be tracks out there even in the asphalt,' she said. She turned abruptly and walked to the door, then turned. 'How about coming over to my place for dinner tonight? I'm not such a bad cook.'

She disturbed him in more ways than one – and that was all right, he thought. If only they could get this business of her suspicions regarding the Peace Engineers straightened out.

Her remark about the shipping department annoyed him. He *had* wondered about the distribution of the interocitors, but had been too busy to do much inquiring about the sale of them. Certainly a good many of them were being turned out, and he didn't have the faintest idea where they went.

He glanced at the interocitor and at the clock. Lunch time – he should have asked Ruth to go with him. Maybe he'd meet her in the cafeteria.

On the way his curiosity won out. He detoured to the shipping room and dock. Outside the big doors the warmth of the sun was drying the freshly wet landscape. He looked around. He couldn't see any tracks and didn't expect to. The loading area was newly constructed and the asphalt firm.

There was one bad spot, however, that drew his notice. Thirty feet out from the dock a pool of water had collected in a saucerlike depression about twenty feet wide. Have to get that leveled up, he thought.

He didn't see Ruth at lunch, and hurried through the meal to get back to the lab. Once there he settled down again before the interocitor and began work. He got out all the books they had given him on the math behind the machine.

He scarcely moved through the remaining hours of the day as he pored over them. He had to admit that Ruth's fear was slowly convincing him there was something he didn't know about the interocitor – and should.

At nine-thirty that night the phone rang. Even as he picked it up, glancing at the clock, a wave of regret passed over him.

It was Ruth's voice that spoke to him. 'Dinner – remember? It's getting pretty cold.'

'Ruth! I've been working here ever since you left. I forgot all about it.'

'That's a nice compliment. The first time I invite you to dinner you forget it.'

'Ruth, I'm awfully sorry!'

'Well, I guessed that's what had happened, so I've packed everything up in an electric warmer. If you're going to be there a while longer I'll bring it over.'

'If you're not careful I'm going to be calling you "darling."'

'Try it and see what happens.'

She hung up before he did.

He returned to his work, but absently. Whatever came of this job, it was worth it to have found her.

It seemed only minutes until he heard her at the door. She bowed formally as he opened it for her. 'Your dinner is served, sir.'

'Golly, Ruth, I don't know what made me forget. I feel like a heel.'

'According to the teachings of psychiatry,' she said, as she began spreading out the dinner, 'people forget only what they want to forget.'

'I can see I've got some rough years ahead of me with a psychiatrist around.'

She turned to him with arched eyebrows. 'Are you thinking seriously of having one around?'

'Mighty seriously, darling – mighty seriously.'

After they had eaten she cleaned up the things and moved towards the door. 'At least I hope you'll take me home now.'

He ran his fingers through his hair and looked back at the machine in its panels by the wall. 'There's just one more thing I want to get through my head. It won't take a minute.'

She slumped in a chair and put her elbow on the laboratory bench. 'So this is the way it's going to be.'

He grinned at her.

For an hour or more he studied the texts on the table in complete silence. Slowly there began to appear a consecutive thread of knowledge that was fundamental in the field employed for communication in the machine. Yet, as it was now built, this basic characteristic seemed to be blanked.

As he nailed down the final factors of it clearly in his mind he straightened up to look at the enigmatic black panels with their shiny indicators and controls. Was this the thing that Ole had stumbled across? He thought of Ruth's description of the boisterous Ole crying hysterically of some vast frightening menace he had seen in the sky, of the thoughts he had heard the Engineer *think* –

If this were it, then perhaps there was something after all in the dread that haunted Ruth and Ole.

Hastily he went over to the interocitor and began removing panels. He reached inside, disconnected a bank of catherimine tubes and reran their input leads. He cut out the visual circuits completely and modified the field strengths in the coils that governed the albion index of the circuits. After half an hour he was finished.

He hesitated a moment before he turned the power into the modified circuits. He glanced at Ruth. Her head was down on the table, her dark hair spilling outward like the leaves of some velvet flower. She was sound asleep. Cal smiled tenderly. Everything was going to be all right.

He threw the switch that energized the altered interocitor. He had no clear conception of what he was looking for, but he knew that the fundamental unblanked field described in the texts should now be emanating from the machine.

It was hardly perceptible at first, like a haunting memory. It was neither sound nor sight. The only word that leaped to his mind was – *thought*.

He looked about in sudden concern for Ruth. She had raised her head as if suddenly roused from troubled sleep. He couldn't tell whether she perceived it, too.

He shut his eyes momentarily and attempted to blot out the remnant of physical sound that filtered through the quiet night. Faintly, an image was forming in his mind as if he were imagining a picture under his own initiative. But he knew he wasn't thinking it. It was coming from – *outside*.

The image of Jorgasnovara was in his mind and he was speaking – no, thinking, for there were no movements of his lips. His lined, chiseled face was cast in planes of utter weariness and discontent. His thoughts seemed addressed to someone.

'. . . report we are doing the best possible under the circumstances. Production of plant C is six hundred units. D is about ready. We have four hundred on hand that you can pick up here tonight. If Soccorian outpost goes can we maintain here?'

There was a moment of silence, in which an answer seemed to be coming to the Engineer from some source, but Cal could not get that.

'All right,' the Engineer said at last. 'Near the outer ring? Give me five minutes.'

The thought of Jorgasnovara receded and vanished from Cal's mind. He turned away from the machine.

'That must have been the way it was with Ole,' said Ruth in a hushed voice.

'What he heard must have been different, however,' said Cal. 'This was nothing fearful to drive a man out of his mind.'

'But Jorgasnovara knows things that would. Didn't you feel it – the sense that he knows and has been aware of things of utter terror and frightfulness that a normal mind could scarcely endure?'

Cal nodded slowly. He had felt the same.

'Ole must have heard some of those things,' said Ruth. 'Do you understand what it's all about?'

'No.' Cal shook his head. 'I don't understand a thing. The interocitor is even more of a mystery than I thought. It is capable of making direct mental contact, yet it is overbuilt with a lot of crude visual and audio circuits.

'Tomorrow we'll go to see Ole. If there's anything sinister that he found we'll get it out of him. I knew him pretty well – he may talk to me. If not, perhaps you can persuade him to submit to pentathol treatment. We'll do what we can.

'Until we know for sure I still won't let go of my paradise. You can't realize what it means to someone who's always wanted to do real engineering and has been bogged down in toaster and electric-razor plants all his life. This technology – it's like breathing pure oxygen.'

'And just as likely to make you drunk.'

'Perhaps.'

'Let's get down to the shipping department,' she said. 'He said only five minutes.'

They had to pass through the section where the long

assembly lines were dark and still, and then they came near the shipping department. They heard the sounds together – the rumbling of the great doors that opened to the outside. There were movements and a light inside the shipping room.

'Down here,' whispered Ruth.

Reluctantly, Cal crouched behind a foreman's desk with her. He felt a little ridiculous – spying on his own shipping department.

Then Ruth shook his arm fiercely and her voice was almost a tiny scream. 'Look at it – out there by the platform – Cal, what is it?'

He saw it then. It had been there all the time but in the darkness it was difficult to distinguish.

A vast ellipsoid that towered above the door, as if it were as tall as the three-story plant. Dim lights were visible in the interior of the thing through the port that was open opposite the platform. A gangplank extended between the two.

Cal thought then of the depression he'd seen that noon after the rain. 'So that was the tracks you tried to tell me about!' he said.

Ruth nodded, trembling in the darkness. 'I knew that depression hadn't been there long and I wondered if – something – had been pulled up to the door to take away the interocitors. But I didn't dream of anything like this! What is it?'

'I wish I knew.' But slowly, there was growing the unbelievable conviction that he *did* know. His mind held it back as long as possible.

The Engineer came into view as they watched. A small instrument like a flashlight was in his hands. With it he was towing a chain of heavy interocitor crates, each of which weighed over nine hundred pounds. They were linked together somehow and followed the tiny beam like obedient dogs.

He disappeared into the depths of the mysterious freighter. The stream of boxes followed for minutes until the last one disappeared into the portal. After moments, the Engineer appeared again.

'Come on!' Cal whispered. 'The roof!'

He tugged roughly at Ruth's sleeve. Obediently, she followed, slipping through the darkness, stumbling once or twice on the iron stairway leading to the roof. And then they were outside.

The top of the ellipsoid was still ten feet above the edge of the roof. As they peered over, they heard the sharp clank of the closing doors below.

'We'd better stand back,' said Cal. 'No telling what –'

The massive object grew suddenly misty. Like a faint, transparent film it seemed suspended fragilely in the air. Then abruptly it was gone.

But Cal had seen its going. It had moved straight up at incredible velocity. For a moment Ruth raised her eyes to follow his gaze out into the distant star field, where a fleeting shadow passed across the Milky Way.

Then she buried her face in his shoulder. 'Cal, I'm afraid! What does this mean?'

He made no answer. It was not a thing of terror. A choking sense of awe made it impossible for him to speak. He had witnessed the miracle that he had never dreamed of seeing in his lifetime – and he was part of it! He would know all of it, and make it his.

The Engineers had conquered space.

He understood now the vast secrecy that shrouded their doings, why they held back a knowledge of their motives, their markets, their ultimate ideals.

For how could they tell the fledgling engineers that the interocitors were produced for a market beyond the stars?

9

The desert was dreamlike in the early morning heat. Cal wished he and Ruth had started a couple of hours earlier than they did. They would have been in the outskirts of Los Angeles now.

He glanced down at the face of his companion, who was curled up in the seat beside him. He smiled tenderly as he watched her sleeping figure. She looked more like a college freshman than a skilled psychiatrist burdened with several degrees.

It was little more than six months since Cal had met her there, he thought. In that short time he had worked harder than ever before in his life. He had put the new plant unit of the Peace Engineers into production in Phoenix. He had seen the first of the complex communicators come off the production lines under his direction – those instruments the Engineers called interocitors.

And he had put his diamond on Ruth's finger.

She stirred as the sunlight brightened the desert. Smiling, she turned her head slowly back and forth.

'Oh-h-h – ' she grimaced. 'It's going to be stiff for a week.'

'Good morning, darling,' said Cal. 'Breakfast coffee is almost ready – just around the next bend in the road.'

Ruth glanced at the straight, miles-long stretch ahead and wrinkled her nose at him. 'I'll have mine out of the thermos you didn't want me to bring along.'

She reached behind the seat and brought out the bottle. As she sipped the warm coffee she said, 'What are you going to say to Ole when we find him? Do you have any idea?'

He shook his head. 'It will all depend on how he reacts. If only he could have told us what he knew instead of running away –'

'I wish we were never going back,' said Ruth. Her voice was low, almost inaudible above the hum of the engine. 'I wish we were never going to hear of Peace Engineers again!'

Cal turned. Her eyes were staring far across the desert to the little fence of mountains beyond. They bore the vision of infinite dread that he had glimpsed the first time he had ever seen her.

It was mid-morning when they reached Los Angeles. The Narcissus Radio Company where Ole worked was one of those small outfits scrabbling for a living on the south side of town. Its single building was a wartime jerry-built shack that looked as if it were now forty years old.

'What a rathole!'

Ruth shook her head in dismay. 'I can't imagine an engineer like Ole coming to work here for *any* reason. Did you ever hear of Narcissus Radios?'

'No,' said Cal, 'and very few people ever will either – except radio service men. I'll bet they really turn out some bloopers in here.'

They left the car and entered the building. Two languid typists seemed to be the total office force.

Cal spoke. 'We'd like to see Mr Swenberg of the engineering department.'

One of the girls shifted her gum into the far corner of her mouth and laughed. 'He *is* the engineering department. Go straight on through to the rear. His office is next to the shipping department.'

They passed through a swinging door and found themselves in a dingy assembly room. Twelve girls and a foreman were putting a can full of parts together, which would be boxed and labeled as a car radio.

The foreman came up. Cal said, 'We want to see Mr Swenberg.'

'Right back there.'

They could see Ole's figure now in the glare of light coming through a door at the rear of the building. He looked up as they approached. His face registered impulsive gladness and then a cold dismay clouded his eyes.

'Hi, Ole!' said Cal. 'We finally decided to come over and inspect this rat's nest you left paradise for.'

Ole took his hand. 'It's a rat's nest, all right. You ought to see our inspection department. The last girl on the line plugs the sets in. If she can tune in KFI the thing goes in a box. I warn you, don't ever buy Narcissus radios – even if I do design them myself.'

'Would you be willing to recommend anything else that you've helped design lately?'

'Such as what?'

'Such as interocitors.'

Ole hesitated. His face seemed to go slack, and his eyes held a beaten look.

'I'd just as soon not talk about *that*.'

'It's what we came for, Ole. We've got to talk about it. Ruth and I – we've found out something new for ourselves. We've got to know what made you run away.'

'What have you found out?' Ole asked, but his face showed no real interest.

Cal wondered if he should say it, if Ole could understand that he actually meant it. 'They've got space flight,' he said slowly. 'We saw their ships – one of them. It picked up a load of interocitors two nights ago and went off – somewhere. It was a spaceship. I'm absolutely certain of that.'

Ole looked narrowly into Cal's eyes. 'I suppose it's

possible. If it's true, it makes it worse than ever. They'll have their way whenever they come out in the open and let the rest of the world know what they intend to do.'

'Did you find out who they are?' said Cal. 'Is that why you left?'

Ole shook his head. 'It was just like sitting on a time bomb, never knowing when it might go off – or even if it would go off at all while I was there. I had to get out.'

Ruth spoke up for the first time. 'Ole, don't you remember that day when you came to my office?'

He looked blank, then slowly shook his head. 'What do you mean?'

'That day you came in babbling about something that had terrorized you. Warner came right afterwards and wouldn't let me do anything for you, but he took you away. The next time I saw you, you said you were leaving to take this job.'

'I don't know what you're talking about. I remember telling you I was leaving, but nothing about the other.'

Suddenly, he waved his palm in front of him as if to brush the whole affair away. 'I've told you I don't want to talk about any of that ugly business over there. I'm through with it! You can go on thinking what you like about it, but I want nothing to do with it – and as long as you're a part of it I want nothing to do with you either. If that's all you came to talk about you may as well go.'

'Ole – !' Ruth began.

Cal touched her arm. 'I'm sorry, Ole. We're disturbed about things ourselves and we thought you might be able to help by telling us about that day you came to Ruth's – '

'I don't know what you're talking about! Now, will you please leave?'

They turned and moved slowly back through the dingy assembly room. No one spoke as they went out of the building. In the car, Cal laid a carton on the seat between them.

'Cal – ' Ruth said, 'we've got to find a way to do something for Ole. He's under terrific tension. He's being torn by some inner conflict that he can't endure much longer.'

'Maybe we'll find the answer in this.' He tapped the carton as he turned the car out into the stream of traffic.

'What's that? You didn't have anything when we went in there.' Then Ruth turned it over and read the printing on the carton. 'You took one of their radios! How did you get it?'

'Used to do sleight of hand in college,' he said. 'I don't think anyone saw me pick it up. I'd rather Ole didn't know it.'

'Why did you take it?'

'I don't know for sure, but didn't you notice how anxious Ole was to get us out of there?'

'How could I help notice being ordered out?'

'But did you stop to figure out why?'

'That's obvious. The tension – our bringing up the Peace Engineer trouble again – '

Cal patted her hand. 'Look, darling. Sometimes there's a disadvantage in being a very brilliant psychiatrist. You need the talents of a dub who's an old solder-slinger from way back. Didn't you notice that back room behind the one we were in?'

'Not particularly.'

'He had an interocitor in there.'

'An int – ! You mean he – ?'

'He'd been working on it just before we came in. I could see the rosin vapor rising from his soldering iron. He had parts of it strung all over the bench, but I know an interocitor when I see one.'

'He didn't want us to see it!'

'That's why I wanted to get out with one of these things instead of standing around arguing with him. He very definitely didn't want us to see it. Anybody else – it wouldn't matter because they wouldn't know what it was. But our coming really gave him the jitters. Here's a good stopping place.'

He swung the car to the curb on a residential dead end street where little traffic flowed. He turned to the box on the seat and ripped it open. With a screwdriver from the glove compartment he removed a panel from the set and grunted softly. 'That's no more a car radio than it is a dishwasher.'

'You mean it's something – like an interocitor, maybe? But Ole wouldn't be doing that. He's not *with* them!'

'I don't know. What can we believe? But whatever his purpose, he's certainly lying to us – some pretty fat, bare-faced lies. More than half of these components are the kind of stuff that goes into the interocitor. It's part of the Engineers' technique.'

'But, Cal, that can't be. He sounded as bitter towards them as ever. He can't be with them still.'

Cal shook his head. 'It looks as if instead of leaving them, he has actually been promoted to a job like Jorgasnovara's on a smaller scale. Why he should be lying to us now I don't know. But I'll bet a nickel he runs the whole place back there.'

When Ruth finally spoke again her voice was thin with fear. 'I suppose you think this means everything is just swell, that Ole has joined them and so it proves that you were right.'

'Ruth, please don't talk like that.'

'I'm sorry. I'm scared, Cal. You didn't see Ole that day he came babbling to me about what he'd heard the Engineer thinking.'

'I don't think everything is all right. I don't see why he lied to us. It makes less sense than ever.'

'What are you going to do? Are you going back to see Ole, or tell Jorgasnovara you know about the spaceship?'

He put the box on the back seat and drew her close with his arm about her shoulders. 'What do you think I should do?'

'Forget about going back. Let's stay here and never go near the place again. What they've done to Ole they could do to any of us.

'He's not himself. I think they put him under some kind of impressed influence that's made little more than a robot out of him. He's their slave, turning out these devices for whatever purpose they have.'

'You don't really believe that, darling. There's a rational explanation that will be perfectly reasonable when we understand it.'

He felt the trembling of her shoulders beneath his arm. He stared down the sunny Los Angeles street. A half dozen kids were riding tricycles on the sidewalk.

They could live on a street like this, he thought. They could have a house like one of these, and their kids could be playing here in the sun in a few years.

It was tempting.

He withdrew his arm and turned on the key again. 'They've got space flight,' he said. 'We know it, and that alone would keep me from backing out now. Why, that ship of theirs was so far beyond the clumsy rockets our militarists have been toying with –

'It speaks of a technology in which the pioneering is over. It could make trips to the stars with safety and regularity.

'And, Ruth – *I want to go to the stars.*'

His own sudden vehemence startled him. He looked into her eyes a moment, then spoke more quietly. 'It's a dream I had when I was a kid. I thought maybe when I was grown up – I haven't even thought about it for years. And now, suddenly, it's possible. I've got to find out about it. If they're withholding it from the rest of the world I'm going to find out why it can't be given out.'

'Yes – of course you will go,' she said quietly. 'But first you will find out who the Peace Engineers are. You will find out the pieces of the picture that they have kept hidden from us.'

He nodded. 'That's what makes it so devilishly hard to understand – their elusiveness. Jorgasnovara told me enough so that up to a point I can understand it. But beyond that point it makes no sense at all.'

'And you have reached that point?'

'This business with Ole pretty accurately defines it.'

'Are you going back there?'

'No.' He shook his head slowly. 'I think the answer still lies in Phoenix – in the interocitor. Why is Ole using one? I want to know more about this apparent thought reading property the machine has. No. I'm going back to work as if nothing had happened and go on from there.'

10

The long, lonely four-hundred-mile drive back to Phoenix ended in late evening. Cal let Ruth out at her place and kissed her good night.

He turned the car north again and drove slowly toward the mysterious plant beyond town. Crouched on the desert with only a scattering of lights, it was like a sleeping monster that he dared not waken.

He could accept Jorgasnovara's explanation of the Engineers' existence, their purpose and their secrecy, he thought. He could understand their withholding full explanations until he proved himself.

But the one wholly illogical factor was Ole Swenberg. Cal could not comprehend why the engineer, who had so bitterly denounced the organization, who had come to Ruth in such panic over some discovery he'd made concerning it – he could not understand how Ole could now be in obvious charge of a small Peace Engineers' plant.

And, though Ole was still using and working with interocitors, he refused to talk about it with Cal – and with Ruth, who had so keenly shared his distrust of the Peace Engineers. It made no sense whatever.

Before he had seen the Engineers' ship Cal had been so sure that everything was all right, that the Peace Engineers had a legitimate reason for secrecy.

Now nothing seemed right. Ole, who had been so bitter against them, was directing a midget plant for them. And he didn't want Cal or Ruth to know about it.

Wearily, Cal turned into the driveway of his own

company-owned house. He felt exhausted beyond endurance. Tomorrow would be time enough for new questions.

In the morning, he returned to the offices and laboratories. It was the same familiar surroundings that he had known for many months, but somehow none of it seemed the same now. He caught himself looking furtively about. He felt watched.

Angrily, he shook off the sensation. He knew it had no basis in reality. It was only the product of his new attitude of suspicion towards the Peace Engineers.

There seemed to be endless details of production to attend to that morning, but by eleven o'clock the assembly lines were rolling smoothly and he managed to get away to his own laboratory.

He locked the door behind him and leaned against it a moment. Would there ever be an end to the questioning in his mind? His doubts fought with his desire to believe that this was the professional paradise he had hoped for – where he could study and work in the freedom that he had always dreamed of –

But Ole had dreamed such dreams – and something had happened to them.

With a savage gesture he strode to the interocitor panel he had reconstructed.

He turned on the power and stood in front of the panel, watching the instruments. He closed his eyes, trying to recover the sensation of telepathic eavesdropping he had experienced before, but nothing came except his own threshing, uncertain thoughts. He half-wondered if he had dreamed that he had heard and seen Jorgasnovara through the instrument, but he knew it was real enough. Ruth had seen and heard, too.

Abruptly, a surge of power emanated from the machine like a voice of thunder – but there was no sound.

He shuddered and pressed his eyelids fiercely. In his mind, he thought. Direct contact from mind to mind without sight or sound. He listened to the thoughts that came and watched their elusive images.

But it was not Jorgasnovara, the Engineer. It was someone reporting to him. '. . . six Secorian colonnades lost. General Planners have decided on resurgence in that sector since it has become our weakest area.'

And then Jorgasnovara's thoughts surged in.

Cal grasped his head involuntarily at the impact of terrible emotion that was hurled from the machine and buried like a million tiny bolts of flame in the cells of his own brain. The whole spectrum of human feeling seemed alive with tortured, throbbing power.

'When will it end?' the thought came. 'When will it ever end?'

Cal searched through the blast for the individual currents of feeling. He sensed a vast homesickness, a longing for peace and confinement to a small spot of land. But strongest of all, a terrifying, overpowering hatred, a hatred reserved only for an enemy whose power has destroyed everything dear. Jorgasnovara hated that kind of enemy, and it seemed to Cal that the power of that hatred alone could destroy life.

Then there came a calmer thought. 'You are tired, Jorgasnovara. You should have let yourself be relieved long ago. There are others who could see this facet of the project through to completion. You have done excellently, but you are not indispensable.'

'A matter of days now,' said the Engineer. 'Only a matter of days, and I shall be ready to relinquish my place.'

'As you will. But you will soon be needed in another place, I am informed. You will have little chance to rest.'

'Rest! Who can rest in the death-struggle of a universe?'

'You are too sensitive. You should have something done about that. You know that our lifetimes will not see the end of the struggle.'

'But we can act as if it would be so.'

There was no answer, but the vision of Jorgasnovara's thoughts remained.

Jorgasnovara's mind seemed to pass slowly over events of some near or distant past. There were glimpses of strange lands that Cal did not recognize – he wondered momentarily if they might be other planets.

Then, upon a sunny landscape, it seemed, a vast roll of darkness burst out of space and over the whole earth and the planets beyond. From Jorgasnovara, there was the sensation of terror and dismay. And then hate.

The hate grew once again to such mighty intensity that Cal could scarcely endure its presence. Slowly it receded, and there was the vision of ships. Mighty ships of space such as Cal had seen that night by the loading dock.

Ships that went up by the thousands against that roll of darkness out of space – and vanished in the flame of their own consuming. He seemed to see endless days and years of fruitless battle; and then the darkness receded, pressed hard by the vast hordes.

And that was the present, Cal sensed. There was battle, and it was not won, and fleets of ships and endless tons of material were swallowed in the daily gorge of war. There, the thought visions ended.

It was moments before he realized that he was no longer receiving the thoughts of the Engineer. The interocitor was still operating, but nothing came to Cal's mind.

He moved at last from a half-crouching position before the bench. His body was bathed in sweat. His brain felt numb from the pummeling of that wave of impressed thought and emotion. Like a flood, the answers to a thousand mysteries poured through his mind and left a thousand more to be answered.

He moved to the phone and called Ruth. 'Come over at once,' he said. 'I know what it's all about.'

He sat down on a laboratory stool while he waited for her coming, and tried to quiet his nerves.

She came, breathless from running. 'What is it?' she asked.

Cal nodded to a chair and stared at the interocitor. Slowly he told her what he had just witnessed.

She seemed uncomprehending. 'This battle – these ships of space destroying each other – I don't understand.'

'War. A more deadly and terrible war than any we could have dreamed of. That's what it means,' said Cal soberly. 'These Peace Engineers – what a ghastly joke their name turned out to be! They have become involved in a full-scale war.

'Who or what the enemy is, I don't know, but the Engineers are attempting to fight it alone. The Earth at this moment is involved in interstellar warfare, and only this handful of men know it. That explains the secrecy!'

'It's hardly possible,' breathed Ruth. 'If these Peace Engineers should fail – why don't they come out and enlist the whole world with them? How did it begin? What is the fighting for?'

'I don't know any of those answers,' said Cal wearily. In his mind he seemed to see again those flaming ships.

'But it's easy to picture how it might have started. For many years they may have carried on secret flights until their ships came to a high state of perfection. Caught by surprise, perhaps, they encountered the first representatives of another planetary culture. Maybe one of our Solar planets, maybe from across the galaxy. But somebody blundered – and there was conflict.

'And rather than risk revealing their secrets, the Engineers are willing to risk all mankind in their effort to fight it out alone.'

Ruth said finally, 'What are we going to do?' It was like the sound of a small child in a vast and lonely cavern.

11

He put his arm around her shoulders, and they stood by the window looking out over the plant and the desert beyond. It was like the last terrible moments before waking from a nightmare, Cal thought. In just a moment now it should be over –

But it wasn't. It never would be as long as he lived. That surging hatred from Jorgasnovara would never leave his mind.

'I keep thinking of Ole,' he said. 'I wonder if he knows of this? Did they tell him about it that day he came to your office? And is that why he is quietly producing war materials in that broken-down shop of his? That would explain why he threw us out of his place. He couldn't tell us why he'd reversed his violent feelings, or even that he had done so.'

'You think that all of this production is war material?'

'What else?' He ran a hand through his thick shock of hair and laughed sharply. 'And I was the guy who was so fed up with practising science in the service of the warriors!'

He turned to the interocitor panel and smacked his hand against it. 'I wonder what this thing *really* does – destroy armies by turning them into idiots, or something equally beautiful from a militaristic standpoint?'

'Stop it, Cal,' said Ruth quietly. 'Stop it!'

He faced her. 'All right. I promise I won't go off like that again. The immediate problem is what do *we* do? Do we go along and help or do we try to throw wrenches in the machinery?'

'How can we do anything but help if what you say is true? I think we ought to see Jorgasnovara and make him lay all his cards on the table.'

'You think he would be willing to do just that?'

'Why not?'

'I don't know. Perhaps if Ole came in this same way they would welcome us. On the other hand, I can't believe he would be very happy about our eavesdropping on his mental processes.'

'You said the other night that he must know.'

'No, I think not now. I don't believe he would have let us go on this way if he did. I think we've discovered this quite accidentally, and that no one knows anything about it.'

'And Ole.'

'I wonder – ' Cal began. He looked speculatively at the panels surrounding him. 'Warner contacted him the first time through the interocitor. I wonder if Ole – '

He advanced to a panel and threw in the power relay again. Ruth watched the familiar glow of the tubes lighting up. Like the candles of some ritual to the gods of science, it seemed to her.

Then Cal started back, his eyes on the meters in sudden fear.

'Someone has activated this – been spying on us while we've talked!'

'Is that possible?'

'Under normal quiescent conditions of the machine – '

There were meaningless flashes of light and color across the bright tube that formed the screen, but nothing recognizable came.

'Do you think you can reach Ole's machine?'

'It's just possible. I may be able to excite his – '

A swirling shape seemed to be growing out of the mist

on the screen. Slowly the lines and planes of a room appeared, a vaguely familiar place.

'That's his laboratory!' exclaimed Ruth.

Then, suddenly, there appeared a face, blurred and out of focus. But there was no doubt about whose it was. A harsh voice barked at them.

'Tighten the beam, you fool. Do you want every machine in the plant excited?'

Cal made a quick adjustment and the blurry image came into focus.

On the screen Ole passed a hand wearily over his face. 'I'm sorry. I'm pretty well wrought up, I guess. I've been watching you for days. I guess I know which side you're on, now.'

'What are you talking about?' said Cal.

'When you came over here I was afraid you might be part of Jorgasnovara's secret police. I couldn't tell whether you were spying on me or not. I had to stay in character as you knew me. I didn't dare say a word. But I've been watching you while you found out what a mess they've got us into. I know now that you're not one of the inner circle yet.'

'Did you know about this war all the time?' asked Cal.

'Yes. That's what nearly drove me crazy, and made me leave the plant. Only I saw more of it than you did. I listened in while Jorgasnovara was getting a direct report from one battle sector. Our little wars are like neighborhood kids brawling in the street compared with the way they fight.'

'What is it all about? How did it start? Why is it so undercover?'

'I don't know for sure, but I think it's about as you guessed it, a blunder when they first contacted some other world, and now they're trying to carry off the fight without letting the rest of the world in on it. I think I know the why of that. Can't you picture the public response to such information?'

'I don't understand your actions. You're working with them. Why should you be afraid I was spying on you?'

'I'm *not* with them – and I think Jorgasnovara knows it. His spies have been here before. They've got to be stopped. Can't you see that?'

'I'm not so sure – now,' said Cal slowly. 'Their enemies might wipe out our entire planet. It looks as if only the Engineers stand between us and destruction. I can't see how we can do anything but throw in with them for all we've got – regardless of our feelings about war. We're in it – but good.'

'Meacham, the Pacifist!' said Ole bitterly. 'There's no reason to believe they'd wipe us out. Maybe they'd like it brought to an end just as much as we would. At least, until we find out, we've no basis for believing otherwise.'

'Have you anything but wishful thinking as a basis for believing that?'

'Yes – I was here for a year before you were. I know Jorgasnovara. He would never ask quarter from anybody. Regardless of the rightness of the cause, he'll fight to the complete destruction of his enemy or himself. If it were his own private war I wouldn't care what happened to him, but he's involved the whole human race.'

Cal recalled that burning hatred of Jorgasnovara. 'It's a question of how we can best get out of this. I can't understand it. It looks like the action of some utter fools, yet they can't be. Their science – '

'It has been pretty well demonstrated that technological sense is not synonymous with social and political acumen.'

'That's the whole thesis upon which Jorgasnovara claims the organization is based – and they seem to be living proof of it – but hardly in the way they intended.'

'Up to now,' said Ole, 'I've been alone. I've been

waiting and hoping for you to show your hand. I dared not reveal what I knew because of his spies.

'He told me about his secret war when I stumbled onto it through the interocitor. He offered me a chance to go along with them, and I was afraid not to.

'That is why I took over this small outfit for him here. I don't even know what this gadget is we're making. I had to gain time until I could find someone else in the organization whom I could trust – and I was hoping it would be you. You've got to help me find some way to stop this thing before it's too late.'

'We're agreed on the ultimate goal of getting out of this mess they've started, but can we compromise on the means for the time being? Let's not try to interfere with their production until we know more. I could do plenty to interrupt production of interocitors – temporarily. But they'd soon replace me when they found out I couldn't keep up,' Cal said.

'All right,' Ole agreed. 'I am coming over for a conference in a couple of days. Since I'm the only one that knows about the war officially let me see what I can do towards pumping Jorgasnovara. You two keep out of the way, and don't say anything until we find out if somebody is liable to get hurt. In the meantime keep glued to your modified interocitor.'

'Do you think he knows we're listening in?'

'I don't know. It's possible he does. He's careless about using his own machine on a loose beam. He may be waiting to smack us down like flies as soon as we make a false move, but we've *got* to take that chance.'

Cal Meacham did little work the remainder of that day. After Ruth left he paced the floor of his laboratory.

The double identity involved in this whole set-up seemed increasingly fantastic. Altogether there were nearly four thousand persons working at the plant. Most of them were simply assemblers hired in Phoenix who didn't know a resistor from a spark gap in the first place. To them the place was simply an electrical manufacturing plant and a weekly paycheck.

To the engineers hired through the idealistic lures of the group, it was a place of intellectual freedom where a super-technology had flowered and was still growing and developing.

And to Jorgasnovara and his inner circle it was a war center. But who composed the inner circle of the Engineers? Who had complete knowledge of the purpose of the plant?

Of all those Cal had met, only Jorgasnovara and Warner had betrayed any such knowledge. Of the others, each man seemed possessed of a single piece of knowledge that was a fragment of the gigantic puzzle. He was given only as much as would fit him into place in that puzzle.

The complacency of his fellow engineers in accepting the place at face value irritated Cal. Yet he almost laughed at his own original willingness to do the same – until he had discovered the unsuspected properties of the interocitor.

It was worse than useless to try to talk to any of the other engineers, he thought. There were several hundred, and to sound them all out would take an endless amount of time that he did not have.

To come face to face with Jorgasnovara and demand information seemed the most foolhardy procedure of all. Yet it seemed the most obvious, since Ole was already in Jorgasnovara's confidence to some degree.

Ole came over in one of the pilotless planes. There were six of these, Cal had learned, and they were in almost constant flight. Besides them, the company used three small planes with conventional controls, and the transport that was Jorgasnovara's private ship.

Ole and Cal went directly to the latter's laboratory. Ruth came in a few moments later. Her face was lined with the strain of having knowledge of the unseen conflict that raged in the heavens.

'Wouldn't it be better for us not to approach Jorgasnovara until we try to find out more by other means?' she asked.

'There's not much chance of it,' said Cal. 'None of us are what you would call cloak and dagger men and it would take long months of that sort of stuff to get anywhere. I think there is a very good possibility that Jorgasnovara will lay his cards on the table and invite us to have a piece – or else. Particularly since he brought Ole into it as he did.'

'Suppose I stowed away,' said Ruth. 'One of the interocitor packing cases could be fitted out nicely. I'm small enough for one.'

'That's nonsense!' said Cal. 'It might be possible to learn a good deal – but the chance of getting the information back would be almost zero. We've got to make contact here, where we've got some kind of leverage.'

'What do you mean?'

'We've got the whole world on our side – and we can do a pretty quick job of letting it know what information we've got already – provided it comes to that.'

'Not if Jorgasnovara decides to throw a quick net around all of us.'

'That's why I'm going to see him alone – and you keep out of it,' said Ole. 'If anything happens to me you had better take what information you've got and head for Washington. It's the only chance I see. I'm due over there in a few minutes. I'll come back as soon as I'm through.'

They watched as he crossed the dusty terrain between buildings. Then Cal turned back to his interocitor and switched on the modified circuits. He adjusted it finely, but he could not excite Jorgasnovara's instrument. The Engineer had it blocked against outside excitation.

Ruth sat by the window, staring out at the bleak desert landscape in the distance.

'Penny – ' said Cal.

She turned slowly. 'Do you trust Ole?' she asked suddenly.

'Trust? What are you talking about?'

'Does it make sense – his being in charge of that small plant over there, and trying to tell us he's opposed to Jorgasnovara? I can't forget how he looked that day after Warner took him away. I can't get over my conviction they did something to put him under their control.

'Isn't it possible that he's just what he said he feared we might be – a spy for Jorgasnovara?'

Cal grinned and put his arms around her. 'How about me? Are you sure you can trust me?'

'Cal – I'm serious. I feel we can't trust anybody. Let's gather up some of the evidence that's available. Let's take samples of components, pictures, and so on, and turn them over to Army Intelligence. Let's take them to the White House if necessary. We've got to let someone else know about this. If Ole should be forced to betray us we wouldn't have a chance!'

'Take it easy, darling. We will – if necessary. But we can't go at it blindly. You don't know the Army. I had dealings with the brass during the war. You don't just go up and say, "Mr General, some guys out here are running a private war that you ought to know about. They're fighting somebody on another planet." That would be the quickest way to a private suite in the booby hatch I know of.'

'Ole is not the same as he used to be. I know it. And I keep thinking that they can do the same to us that they have done to him.'

He took her arm and led her towards the door. 'Let's go down to the cafeteria for a snack and forget about it for a while.'

'No, I'd better get back to my office. There are two new engineers due this afternoon. If I'm away from my office very long Warner will think something's up. Call me as soon as you hear from Ole.'

'Okay – and quit your worrying.'

She gave him a faint smile and went out the door.

12

Cal turned to his benches and equipment. It was useless to try to work. His mind spun uncontrollably about the thing they had uncovered. It was like fighting an unknown assailant in the dark. There was nowhere to get a grip on the problem.

He wondered if Ole would blunder in talking with Jorgasnovara. He had his own secret fears that Ruth might be right about Ole. What would the Engineer's reaction be? Cal tried to imagine how the conversation was going, to reconstruct it in his mind –

The desert shadows grew swiftly longer. Cal watched the clock impatiently. At last, with a start, he realized that Ole had been gone nearly four hours. It was almost quitting time at the plant. He went to the phone and buzzed Jorgasnovara's secretary before she left.

'I'd like to know if Mr Swenberg is still in conference,' he said. 'I want to see him before I leave.'

The girl was silent for a moment as if checking her memory. 'Mr Swenberg left quite some time ago for his own plant. He stayed only ten or fifteen minutes. But he left a message for you that he had to leave right away and would see you next time he came over.'

Cal hung up slowly. Outside the window the heat haze on the desert swirled like a copper river. He felt stifled and smothered.

His phone buzzed. It was Ruth.

'Cal? I wanted to call you before I leave. I'm being given a new assignment at another plant, and it's necessary for me to leave right away. I can't tell you anything about it, and I won't be able to see you for some time, but you'll hear from me. I'm sorry it has to be so suddenly. I'll see you soon.'

'Ruth! Wait!'

He stopped. It was obvious that she was not alone. She was saying what she had been told to say. They had her trapped.

'It's all right, darling,' she said. 'Everything's all right. The plane is taking off soon. 'Bye, now.'

She hung up.

He stood motionless, staring. Ole's attempt had triggered Jorgasnovara into swift action. They had Ole – now Ruth.

He'd be next, Cal thought. But there wasn't time to consider that. He had to get to Ruth.

He raced down the stairs and through the corridors of the building. His running footsteps echoed on the asphalt walks between buildings.

He entered Ruth's office, and found it empty. Her desk was neatly tidied as if she'd left for the night. Where had she called from, he wondered. Why had they let her call at all?

He turned to the window and looked out at the airfield. In front of the hangar, one of the pilotless ships was being warmed up. Ruth was walking towards it, Warner beside her. Cal choked back an exclamation, and ran from the room. He felt somehow that if she went up in that plane she would be gone from him forever.

She had climbed in, and a mechanic slid the canopy shut as Cal raced along the apron. With a sudden roar the motor was gunned and shot back a sandblast into his face. He ran on, vainly trying to overtake the rolling plane.

It moved to the runway. He ceased his vain running as the plane swiftly grew smaller. It shrank to a dot in the sky.

He turned then at the sound of a footstep behind him. It was Warner.

'Mr Meacham!' Warner came up and took his hand. 'You saved me a trip over your way.'

'Ruth – ' said Cal.

'Something very special came up this afternoon. Mr Jorgasnovara asked her to take a special assignment for a time. Sorry it wasn't possible to notify you earlier but you needn't worry. She will be quite all right.'

'You wanted to see me?' Cal's mouth felt cottony.

'Yes – we also have something new for you. Mr Jorgasnovara is very pleased with your work and feels that you can assist us in more complex operations which we have under way. However, I will leave it to him to give you the details. He'd like to see you at nine in the morning in his office. Please be sure to be there on time. I'll be seeing you again.'

Warner smiled and walked away.

Cal watched his retreating figure. It was incredible. They were asking him to walk right into it. Did they take him for an utter fool? No. That was not right. They did not underestimate him. They could reach out and take him any moment they chose.

With their damnable technology they could probe his brain and dissect every secret thought. There was no hiding. Why had he supposed for a moment that he and Ole and Ruth could operate in their midst without detection?

He turned again to try to locate that disappearing speck in the sky. It was already gone from sight.

He began walking back towards the plant buildings. Inside, his growing panic turned his stomach into a knot. He wiped his moist hands against his trouser legs. He ought to get out – tonight. He'd have to make a try, at least.

He returned to his lab and drew the venetian blinds. He made doubly sure the interocitors were disconnected, beyond all chance of excitation. Then he began packing. He filled a pair of brief-cases with samples of components: some of the incredible ten-thousand-volt condensers the size of a bead – the ones that had first lured him to the Peace Engineers. He took scores of other small-sized components that were wholly foreign to conventional manufacturing techniques. Then he gathered up some of the booklets containing photographs of equipment and some of the textbooks they had given him.

He surveyed the fat cases and crushed them shut. It would have to be enough. Somewhere between the White House and the Pentagon he'd find some brass that would listen to him.

It was dark now. Later there would be a moon, but for the time being the desert was black with night. He moved slowly and quietly along the corridors of the plant and stepped into the shadows outside. Only the watchmen's lights illuminated the yard, and he stayed in the dimness of these as much as possible.

He paused a score of times in the shadows to look behind and all about. His heightened fear peopled the dark places with unseen pursuers.

He reached the airfield at last. There were half a dozen mechanics and attendants on night duty, including the operators of the giant target beam that guided the pilotless ships. He swallowed to moisten the cotton dryness of his throat and went into the small, brightly-lit office.

The mechanic in charge looked up. 'Hello, Mr Meacham. Going out tonight?'

'Yes. I want one of the manual ships. I have to take a short trip.'

'We could give you one of the automatics, and you could sleep until you get there.'

'No. I have quite a number of short stops to make. I'd better have a manual.'

'Okay. We'll have it rolled out and warmed up in just a few minutes.'

He sat down to wait. Was it his imagination, or were they unnecessarily slow about getting the plane out? He wondered if the mechanic had gone to call Warner or Jorgasnovara for instructions. But it was coming now at last. He heard the rumble of the broad doors of the hangar sliding back and turned to watch them roll the ship out. He picked up his cases and hurried out.

'Warm it up a few minutes for you?' the mechanic asked.

'I'll take it,' said Cal. 'Thanks a lot.'

It was like a dream, he thought afterwards. The white overalled mechanics were like waiting ghosts there in the half-light on the apron. How far were they going to let him go? Which one of them would strike?

But they were starting the engine. It caught suddenly with a hearty roar. He closed the canopy and taxied down to the strip. He gunned the motor and felt the tail lift, then slowly he drew back on the stick and felt the smooth rocking of the airborne ship.

It was unbelievable that he had actually got away. He couldn't believe that he had outwitted the Engineers. They had let him go for some purpose of their own.

But, as the desert merged with mountains and then became desert again, he began to relax and feel the weight of the strain lift from his mind. As he crossed New Mexico, the moon rose and splashed all the earth below with cold light.

He began to think of what he was going to do in Washington, of how he would find someone who would believe his story of a secret group of scientists who had involved Earth in an interstellar war. He began to believe that he would actually get there.

13

It was somewhere between Amarillo and Oklahoma City that he first saw the shadow. He was flying almost directly into the moon when the great, semi-transparent silhouette showed up against the silver disc.

His taut nerves forced an involuntary scream from his throat. He knew that shape – that vast, ellipsoid that he had once seen shooting into space faster than the eye could follow.

He leaned the stick and jammed his foot against the pedal. The ship heeled over in a tight turn at right angles to his former course. There was a long low cloud bank a few miles away in the otherwise clear sky. If he could get into that –

He couldn't know whether they had seen him or not, but fear of pursuit and failure swelled within him again.

If they captured him before he revealed his knowledge of the Peace Engineers there would be no one who could warn of the menace their ambitions and blunders had created.

It was foolish, he thought, to suppose that he could get away. If they were really searching for him he could not hide from so simple a thing as a radar beam. And he knew their technology had given them means far more effective than radar.

But the cloud was less than two miles away, and he fled blindly towards it.

Halfway there, the shadow fell over him. It blotted out the moon and the sky of stars, and he screamed again in terror. The great hull was poised almost above, moving silently with his plane. In panic, he jerked on the stick and jabbed the foot pedal.

But the plane did not swerve. And then the motor coughed and died. He gripped the useless controls while the ship continued in the grip of an invisible force from above.

Slowly the distance between the two ships narrowed. And now Cal saw that a wide hatch had opened in the base of the spaceship, a hatch wide enough to swallow his entire plane.

It drew closer. The border of the opening in the spaceship was dropping past him. He shoved back the canopy for a final glimpse of the silvery earth below. Then the hatch closed and he felt the plane drop upon it, resting on its landing gear.

He sat there for a long moment in utter darkness. There was no sound nor sense of motion. It was a void in which all perception had vanished.

It seemed like the suddenness and finality of death. He had blundered, he thought, from first to last. He had been confused by his wanting to believe in the Peace Engineers at their face value. It had taken him too long to believe that they were anything but what they professed to be.

He tried to think of what his failure might mean – to Ruth and Ole and to the whole human race – but he was too tired to put one thought after another in consecutive order. His failure was too great for comprehension.

Abruptly lights came on. Except for his plane, the chamber was completely bare. He climbed down from the cockpit and stood on the metal plating of the hatch door.

A spaceship, he thought. He was actually aboard a spaceship bound for some unknown destination. But there was none of the anticipated boyhood thrill. There was only dull aching despair within him.

His muscles tensed at the sudden faint sound of an

opening door. He whirled to face it and saw two men entering. Neither was familiar. Their faces were almost expressionless. There was neither animosity nor greeting.

'Please come with us,' said one.

Cal stifled an impulse to let loose a flood of questions. He checked it with the knowledge that it would be useless.

One of them led the way through the door. The other followed Cal. Neither spoke.

They took him down a long metal-walled corridor that reminded him of a battleship. At last they halted before a door.

'Please remain here,' said one as he opened the door. 'This will be yours until we arrive. If you need anything just press this button by the door and we will attempt to serve you. We would advise that you sleep the remainder of the flight. We arrive early in the morning.'

'Where?' Cal could not hold back that one question.

The man looked at his companion, then back at Cal. 'Luna,' he said. And closed the door.

Cal stood there for a long moment, facing the blank door.

Luna –

He turned about. For the first time he saw that the opposite wall had ports that looked out to space. He walked towards them. There was a single moment of vertigo as he glimpsed the scene outside, and he turned his head away. Then, cautiously, he looked back, his hands gripping tightly the back of a chair by the port.

Below him Earth wheeled, a mottled bowl. About seven or eight hundred miles away, he supposed.

For the first time, the full impact of the gap between the technology of the Engineers and the rest of Earth struck him. Down there at White Sands the Army was fitfully thrusting its feeble rockets one or two hundred

105

miles into the atmosphere. No one had succeeded yet in freeing one from Earth's gravity.

But the Engineers' ships were crossing space with the ease and luxury of liners crossing the Atlantic.

Maybe there was a reason for their not asking help from men who had not succeeded in building anything more than an enlarged firecracker. What help could such men be in a battle that raged across the depths of space?

He slept finally. The bed was as soft and luxurious as he could have asked for.

An alarm wakened him and soon afterwards the guides – or guards – of the previous night entered the room. They carried breakfast on a tray.

'We will arrive within an hour. Please be ready. Jorgasnovara requires your presence for a conference.'

'Jorgasnovara! He's aboard?'

'Among others.'

They left, and Cal turned again to the ports. They seemed to be coming in for a wide orbit around the Earth side of the moon. Momentarily his awareness of imprisonment retreated and his senses absorbed the beauty of the vision through the porthole. He picked out the old familiar landmarks – Copernicus, Tycho, the Sea of Serenity, Mare Imbrium –

He saw for the first time the other side of the moon with its shadowy, unfamiliar spires and vast craters. The ship began to descend among those unnamed craters.

Cal strained his sight to detect some sign of habitation. Shadowy twilight gave the effect of a fantastic etching, and hid everything that might be familiar.

The ship had almost touched ground before he saw a widespread group of one-story buildings that lay almost perfectly camouflaged on a flat plain between two giant mountain ranges, higher than anything Cal had known existed on the moon.

106

Beside one section he saw a dozen other ships like the one in which he rode, and four others that were monsters, dwarfing the smaller ships like hens hovering over broods.

The two men came again as the ship touched the surface of the moon. Cal followed them along the same corridor, and then wound through other passages that he sensed were taking him through the width of the ship to the other side. Not once did he see another person.

He observed the airtight causeway that had been extended from the ship to the port, eliminating all need of spacesuits in disembarking.

They came out into the building, and there he saw scores of other people, but none he knew, though he scanned their faces for signs of recognition. The pair who guided him stopped at last before a door.

'Wait here. Mr Jorgasnovara will be here soon.'

He stepped in and closed the door.

Across the room Ole and Ruth were seated.

'*Cal!*' Ruth jumped up and ran towards him. She threw her arms around his neck while he stood rigid, scarcely believing, trying to comprehend what he saw. Then his arms went around her and he held her tight.

Ole came towards them slowly, smiling. 'This is about the last place I expected our next meeting to be.'

'What have they done to you?' said Cal. 'Why are we here? What do they intend to do with us?'

Ole motioned him to a chair by the small polished table at which they had been sitting.

'We misunderstood some of our data,' he said, with sudden bleakness in his face. 'Jorgasnovara has straightened Ruth and me out somewhat. In a way the situation is not quite as bad as we thought. From another viewpoint it is much worse, perhaps.'

'But they are engaged in a war, aren't they? We weren't mistaken in what we overheard regarding that.'

107

'No – we weren't. They're engaged in a war, all right. Our mistake was the assumption that the Engineers are Earthmen.'

Cal stared. '*Mistake!* You mean they are from somewhere else?'

Ole nodded. 'The key men. Jorgasnovara and Warner and many of the others. This whole advanced technology was brought by them. It never developed on Earth at all.'

Cal stared soundlessly, his entire mental concept of the Peace Engineers shifting slowly to this undreamed of possibility.

'Why? What do they want of us? Are they trying to take Earth over for a war base?'

'No, it's not that. We aren't that important to them. In fact they can get along without us.

'They gave Ruth and me their story yesterday. Jorgasnovara was going to pick you up and bring you to the spaceship after he'd given you the basic facts this morning. He wanted us to see their moon base, and let us use an historical instrument they have here.

'But you fouled it all up by jumping the gun and taking off the way you did.

'I warn you that when Jorgasnovara gets through explaining you'll probably want to punch somebody in the nose or else go out and bat your head against a wall – depending on which way your inferiority complex blows.'

'You don't make a bit of sense,' said Cal. He turned to Ruth. 'What's he talking about?'

She smiled, the same kind of bitter, rueful smile he had seen on Ole's lips. 'You'll find out. Here comes Jorgasnovara now.'

The Engineer closed the door softly behind him and stood in front of it for a moment. His eyes locked with Cal's, and seemed to peer into the depths of his being as if trying to plumb the hidden knowledge and feelings that he possessed.

108

14

Cal understood now the feeling of alienness that diffused from Jorgasnovara. It was not hard to think of him as foreign to Earth. He began walking towards the table and consulted his watch. 'I believe our appointment was for nine, Mr Meacham. Dr Warner told me he had arranged with you.'

'He didn't mean these particular arrangements,' said Cal, with faint humor. Somehow he felt a growing sense of ease. He could not erase his initial desire to like Jorgasnovara in spite of the mystery of the man.

'No. We were too busy to pay attention to some of the details of your actions. We did not foresee your attempted escape until you had gone. I'm sorry that it was necessary to subject you to the shock that perhaps resulted from our precipitate method of overtaking you, however, I want to assure you that our purpose is benign.'

'You are at war.' Cal leaned forward abruptly. 'You let us overhear snatches of reports passing between you and others of your group. Why?'

'We wanted you to know about it.'

'To what purpose? If you intend to involve Earth or wanted our help in some capacity why didn't you simply say so?'

'We had to find out about you three. We had to know your reaction. We had to know how much you hate war. So we gave you the clues and watched. Of all those with whom we have worked, your reaction has been most satisfactory. We are ready to ask if you will help us.'

'How? And why? Why should we involve ourselves and Earth in something that is no concern of ours?'

Jorgasnovara hesitated, speculating, as if wondering what kind of analysis Cal could comprehend.

'You have had experience during your own recent World War. You saw how the waves of battle washed back and forth over primitive peoples who had little or no comprehension of who was fighting, or to what purpose.

'You saw these primitive peoples sometimes employed or pressed into service by one side or the other. On the islands of your seas they built airfields for you; they sometimes cleared jungles and helped lay airstrips. They had no comprehension of the vast purpose to which they were contributing a meager part, but they helped in a conflict which was ultimately resolved in their favor.'

Cal's face had gone white. He half-rose from his seat. 'You mean – ?'

Jorgasnovara waved him down. 'This greater conflict of which I have spoken has existed for hundreds of generations. Your people were barely out of caves when it began. It will not be ended in your generation or mine.

'Its center of origin and the present battle lines are far from your galaxy, far beyond the range of your greatest telescope. The people involved and the principles in dispute are far beyond your powers to comprehend. But we need your help.'

'To build an airstrip?'

Jorgasnovara smiled. 'These interocitors which you find so interesting are a small item of communication equipment which is used in some of our larger vessels. There are about a score of other, similar devices being made in different parts of the world. They are simple devices, comparable, say, to your pushbuttons. We need you to make some pushbuttons for us.'

Cal understood what Ole had meant now. He *did* want

110

to punch somebody in the face. Rage, frustrated and impotent, swirled within him. The insolence of this super-race that would hire Earthmen to make their pushbuttons!

Jorgasnovara saw it and his expression grew cold. 'You have a stupid pride that is the greatest hindrance in the progress of your people. Is it of any real importance that there exists a culture to which you can be only makers of pushbuttons? Does that lessen your worth in your own eyes? If it does your values are cheap.'

For a moment Cal hated the Engineer. But his rage began to subside, swallowed up by the infinitely greater wisdom that he glimpsed in the man and the culture of Jorgasnovara.

'There is only one question,' he said at last. 'What is right? Do you have it? Is there any reason we should help you, rather than your enemy, whoever he may be?'

'I think there is,' said Jorgasnovara. He slid back a panel in the table top, which Cal had not noticed before. Some kind of instrument panel lay exposed. In a receptacle were several pairs of helmets with cords leading to the panel. Jorgasnovara passed them around the table.

'This is why I brought you three to this base on your moon. You have to see what I am about to show you in order to understand.'

They examined the instruments in their hands. Cal noticed a fine mesh network that covered the skull. Fitting over the eyes were a pair of soft opaque pads. They completely blinded him when the helmet was in place.

Jorgasnovara touched a panel of switches and dials and abruptly there was vision. The three of them *felt* that they had been transported across unthinkable vastnesses. There was starry void all about them. They seemed to be moving, and more swiftly than light they approached one star that slowly swelled to a galaxy, its twin spiral arms a pattern of light against the blackness.

The scene shifted and was replaced by the vision of a planet of that galaxy. There were small cities and vast fields of pleasant color, and the world was peopled by creatures not greatly variant from Earthmen. A sense of peace and contentment of mind filled them as they looked upon that scene.

It was midday when the blackness came. A slow blotting out of light that turned the people's faces skyward and froze them with an unnamed terror. The three Earthlings felt that terror as they watched through the instrument of Jorgasnovara. They felt the incalculable evil and death that was in the blackness shrouding the planet.

Time was condensed, and eons became seconds, and they looked upon the world again. This time it was like an anthill in the wake of a flaming torch. Crisped and blackened, everything that represented sentience and growth and living hope had died. Through all time life could never again flourish upon that world.

They could smell death. Destruction and war shrouded them. It seemed more than they could endure. Cal was aware that Ruth had ripped the helmet from her head. He lifted his own and saw her sitting white-faced and trembling.

'Look again,' said Jorgasnovara.

Once more they were in space, and their vision encompassed a span of light years. As far as they could see, a line of titanic warships flowed through space beyond the speed of light.

And then there was battle. Like a spark it began and ignited the whole of space. Vast forces that twisted and wove the fabric of space itself engulfed the ships, imprisoning them in webs of impenetrable time and space and turning their crews into screaming things that would live forever.

112

Cal hurled the set from his head and wiped his sweating face. Ruth was pale and Ole breathed heavily.

'It is possible,' said Jorgasnovara slowly, 'that the people of your planet would never know that this war had ever raged, regardless of the outcome. You would be of no concern to the enemy. He has higher goals than the conquest of your little world. And my people would never molest you.

'We do not *require* your help, any more than your armies had to have the help of some savage tribe to clear their jungles. You would have won your war. We will win ours.

'But we need you, speaking collectively of all the primitive worlds to whom our emissaries have come. On each of thousands of planets whose people are making whatever items their culture will permit that will be of use to us.

'Some are even building our warships and the mighty generators that warp space about a galaxy. But they do not know to what purpose they are building – only those whom we have commissioned as our agents understand their part in this cosmic effort.

'So that is why I have come to you, Cal Meacham. My predecessors and I have organized the Peace Engineers and carried it on for many decades now. The story I told you was true. Our work spared your planet the devastation of atomic war for many years.

'We have used the products of your greatest men of science. But none have been able to carry on without our direct leadership. We need someone who understands more directly the psychology of Earthmen.

'Will you take charge of our affairs on Earth for the rest of your life?'

Cal had known the question was coming. He had sensed it far ahead of Jorgasnovara's actual voicing of it. Still, it was like a blow that numbed his senses and left him only dimly conscious of the reality about him.

A lifetime of service in a vast effort of war, the whole of which he could never comprehend. He, who had sworn never again to so much as think of an instrument of war, who had hated the scheming and the killing and the designing of scientists for better ways of destroying more of their fellow men. But he thought back to that vision of evil and terror that Jorgasnovara had shown them, and he knew there was only one answer.

'Yes,' he said slowly. 'I'll help you.'

He knew that the things he had seen were true. He knew that Jorgasnovara had not lied, that his people were combating a vast force that would destroy the hope of endless races of sentient life on countless planets.

But that did not assuage his despair.

'When will it ever end?' he said in a voice that was almost a whisper. 'Will there ever be a time when sentient beings will not murder their own kind?'

Then he remembered that he had once heard Jorgasnovara thinking that same despairing thought. Their eyes met in a look of common understanding.

'Sometime,' the Engineer said. 'Sometime there will be an end to the destruction and killing. But come, it is past lunch time. Let us enjoy a meal together.'

It was midnight when the spaceship landed again beside the plant. It paused only long enough for the three to get out of the way of its crushing field and then it vanished into the night sky again.

Cal put his arm about Ruth as they stood there looking up at the moon.

'It didn't happen,' said Ole. 'I'll swear it didn't.'

From somewhere they heard the sound of a car as someone drove in from a late show in Phoenix. All about them the prosaic shadows on the desert and the sounds of night lent unreality to the things that they had seen and heard.

Cal looked up at the stars. He thought of the battle that raged beyond the farthest of them. The light of the suns that illumined that field of battle would not reach Earth for thousands of millennia. Perhaps Earth itself would be cold and dead after those eons had passed. Was such a war any concern of his?

The evil that Jorgasnovara had shown them was timeless. It was the concern of every being in all creation, thought Cal. As long as it existed there would be no absolute freedom for anyone. And his life would be well spent in working with the forces that Jorgasnovara represented.

He took Ruth's hand and started along the walk. 'Let's go. It's getting late, and tomorrow we've got to make a lot of – pushbuttons.'

15

Two days later Jorgasnovara called Cal from the moon base as he had promised, to give the full story of the group with which Cal had now allied himself. Throughout the morning and well into the afternoon Cal sat before the interocitor letting the flow of thoughts from the Engineer wash through his own mind.

Jorgasnovara belonged to the Llannan Council, an organization of worlds from more than a hundred galaxies. In the Council chambers mutually alien life forms sat to resolve the difficult problems of learning to live together. The greatest problem of all their long history was the one that Jorgasnovara had revealed to Cal, the problem of combating the vast and able enemy who had swept out of the depths of space to conquer all life that stood in its way. There was no telling how many galaxies had been overrun in how many eons of time by that enemy.

The Llanna knew very little of the origin of the creatures they fought. There seemed to be an alliance somewhat like their own between wildly variant members of numerous galaxies. This alliance called itself the Guarra, and it was evident that no one had ever successfully halted its sweep of destruction except the Llannan Council.

A few of the Llannan worlds were inhabited by beings closely resembling Earthmen. Jorgasnovara's own planet was one of these, and from it had been selected the technicians to initiate the work of drawing Earthmen into alliance with the Council.

It was recognized that it would be hopeless to openly

invite Earth to participate. The scope of the conflict was too vast. Earth's responsibility was too remote for its people, generally, to grasp the need for participation. It was as Jorgasnovara had said: 'Earth is an island, which can be by-passed completely, or temporarily occupied if need be.'

In the latter case it would be rocked by the thunder of this mighty inter-galactic warfare. But Earthmen, like the islanders of their own seas when Earth's wars swirled about them, had no capacity for understanding the power and depth of the forces involved.

Llannan emissaries and technologists, therefore, had set up manufacturing plants in a score of nations, as they had done on thousands of other worlds which could not participate in open conflict. On each planet they tried to conform to the psychological requirements of the inhabitants. In the case of Earth, they had set up the Peace Engineers ideal, which had attracted Cal.

Jorgasnovara's face was tired as he finished his story over the interocitor.

'I don't know whether we have done a very good job or not,' he said. 'I have often felt that we have not handled this Peace Engineers program as effectively as we might have. It has been very difficult to select any motivation whatever by which we might draw your interest.

'I will be very honest. We do not understand your people. We can't predict what you will do with anything like the degree of accuracy possible among our own. Your irrationalities make it appear as if there is no trustworthiness to be found on your planet, but we know this is not so. We know you have difficulty in understanding yourselves, your own unpredictability, and we have done the best we could to work out a program adapted to it. But I fear that our success has not been exceptional.'

'No,' said Cal. 'When you first came to me with this

Peace Engineers ideal I was ready to accept it wholeheartedly, and I am sure that's the case with most of the other engineers. But it was not followed up.

'That was the first thing that really excited our suspicions regarding your organization. The engineers are restless, the whole staff. There needs to be an organization. The psychology of Earthmen requires a fraternal group, meetings, speeches, and slogans. A continual activity along the general theme of Peace Engineers.'

'We had something of that nature when we were very small, decades ago. It seemed difficult to continue, and when we grew so much bigger we neglected it, mostly because we didn't know how to handle it properly. Knowing your people, do you think it can be done? Or should the whole idea be dropped and something else supplied to take its place?'

'I don't know,' said Cal. 'It's difficult working with a false front. Inevitably it blows up in your face. Despite the rigorous tests you gave us, any active organization of that kind will show up crackpots. On the other hand, it can't continue in the half-hearted way it has been conducted so far.

'I'll make a recommendation, if you wish, after I study it further and confer with Ruth and Ole and some of the engineering staff.'

'I'll leave it to your judgment,' said Jorgasnovara. 'I'm going to leave you for a few months, in which you will have time to study the organization and administration.

'Detailed matters will continue to be handled by the Llannan delegates so you will be free. I want you to evaluate the entire program from an Earthman's viewpoint and let me know where we have erred in dealing with people of your psychology.'

Jorgasnovara closed his eyes briefly and passed a hand over his lined face. 'I have to go to confer with the

General Council,' he continued. 'I am going to try to take a rest, but I fear there will be little time for that.

'You may as well know that the war is going very badly. Our reverses in recent months have been terrible. Production of weapons and equipment must be increased. That will be your main objective, to get a greatly increased production of all the various instruments being manufactured on Earth.'

'Could the war be lost?' said Cal.

The Llannan nodded slowly. 'It could – but it won't. Civilizations in countless galaxies of the universe are depending on us to see that it is not.'

Looking upon the great, tired features of the emissary, Cal felt regret for his doubts about the wisdom of committing himself and Earth's resources to the Llannan battle cause.

Jorgasnovara affected him like that. In the man's presence he understood instinctively what was right and what was wrong. It was only when he was alone with his fears and doubts that questions entered his mind about the propriety of what he had done.

'Do your best,' said Jorgasnovara, after a moment's pause. 'If any real emergency arises you can call my subordinates here at moon base. Also, the administrators of the other manufacturing plants know of your appointment. When I return I will take you on a tour of all Llannan properties.

'Until then I will say good-bye.'

Cal smiled wistfully and nodded as the screen of the interocitor went dark. For a long time he continued to sit in the Engineer's office staring at the dark screen and the factories visible in the desert haze beyond the window.

The Llanna were right, he thought. It was beyond the capacity of Earthmen to comprehend the scope of that great intergalactic battle. But he wondered how great was the capacity of the Llanna themselves to understand all that was taking place. Could any sentient mind think in terms of galaxies by the hundreds, of a conflict involving an enemy from beyond the farthest reaches of Earth's telescopes?

And, he thought bitterly, having conquered such vastness in space and time, why did sentient creatures have to devote their energies to conquest and war and destruction?

Could any of them find the answer to that question?

It was almost dusk when his reverie was broken by Ole's approach from the outer office. Ole had spent the last two days investigating his own new duties as director of the interocitor assembly plant.

He entered the office and sat down across from Cal and wiped a hand across his moist face.

'How did it go?' said Cal. 'Can you handle the production bugs?'

'The Llannan boys can handle those. They don't need any help from us. Sometimes I wonder why they dragged us into this at all on the engineering level.'

'Manpower. They haven't got enough people of their own to do the job. They'll pull out as soon as we're completely ready to take over.'

'I'm beginning to wonder if we can handle the labor end of it.'

'Why?'

Ole shook his head. 'I'm not sure. Probably I'm just worrying about the necessary secrecy of the whole deal – this keeping our own people from knowing where the stuff is going.

'But it seemed like there was something more in the plant today as I walked through it. Maybe it's because I've been away from interocitor assembly for so long that I thought I noticed a difference.'

'What kind of a difference?'

'A feeling. You know how it is when you come into a room where people have been quarreling. I can't put a finger on it. It's ugly, like a mutiny. It smells like strike to me.'

'Strike? What the devil would they want to strike about?'

Ole shrugged. 'What do people ever strike about? Restlessness. A need to express their own importance. We're ripe for it here. They don't know what's going on. It pricks their ego. They can prick back by pulling a walkout.

'I think it's coming, and if it does, this whole thing will be blown wide open. Government officials will be brought into it. It will be impossible to maintain the secrecy of our delivery destination and what we're making here.

'I tell you, Cal, this whole thing has grown too big. It can't be handled the way Jorgasnovara wants to do it. Maybe they can do it that way on most of the other planets where they operate, but not on Earth. Earthmen are too doggoned nosey about something that even smells like mystery or secrecy.'

'Have you talked with the union?' said Cal.

'It hasn't gone that far – yet. I tell you it's just a feeling I've got, but I know it's coming. It's going to blow up in our faces.'

'Figure out some kind of production bonus,' said Cal, 'before they have a chance to complain openly. We hold the upper hand there. We don't have to show a financial profit. The Llanna can pour all the money we need into this project.'

'There'll be some other excuse, then,' said Ole gloomily. 'It won't matter how much money you give them. They just have to strike periodically to show things are still done the democratic way around here, and they're just as good as the next guy.'

'It'll stall them a while, and we need that. I've got to get my feet on the ground. I want to take a tour of all the plants with Jorgasnovara, but it might be two months away. Maybe we can figure out a way to handle it after that, but let's try to stall that long.'

Cal took a tour through the interocitor plant himself the following day. He walked along the huge assembly lines and stopped to chat with the foremen and the girl assemblers. He visited the engineering section, looking over the shoulders of the draftsmen, checking details with the designers who were striving to meet new specifications on the interocitors and other devices.

By noon he had reached his own conclusions. Ole was unquestionably right. Something unpleasant was in the air. He felt it emanate from the working force as he moved among them. The engineers' discontent over the Peace Engineers set-up, he understood, but he should have noticed the atmosphere of the production lines long before. It hadn't built up overnight.

He called a conference with Dr Warner and Ruth Adams the next morning. Warner was a Llannan, a psychologist among his own race, but he was wholly dependent on Ruth for his understanding of Terrestrian psychology. Even Ruth had not known that fact until after Jorgasnovara's revelation.

Warner had relied wholly on her knowledge and advice in choosing the recruits for the engineering staff, at the same time concealing from her his dependence. Now that she understood fully what her position had been, she felt bewildered and a little helpless at its magnitude.

Cal outlined to them Ole's suspicions and his own feelings about the plant.

'It's almost as if the whole thing is on the verge of

breakdown,' he said, 'just as Jorgasnovara has turned it over to us. At the moment I've got to admit, Dr Warner, that I don't see how the secrecy of the project can be maintained much longer. When the break comes, the knowledge of what we are doing will spread in every direction.'

'I think not,' said Dr Warner. 'Take a glance at this, Cal.'

He passed forward a sheet of paper. Cal glanced down and began reading. It was a standard resignation form prepared for those leaving the Peace Engineers. Cal scanned through it, then looked up with a blank stare on his face. He looked helplessly from Ruth to Warner.

The Llannan psychologist pressed a button at the base of the desk lamp beside him. 'Read it again,' he said.

Cal glanced down once more. The sudden gap that had appeared in his mind seemed to close with a swift, rushing flow of knowledge.

'What – what did you do?' he said. 'What happened to me?'

'Selective, induced amnesia. Presentation of this page for a workman or engineer to sign will wipe from his mind all recollection of the things he has learned and done while here. It has been used quite a number of times so far, with very good success. It is a reverse of the process used in the training manuals. I didn't think you had been shown this before.'

'No, I hadn't!' said Cal faintly. The memory of that sudden gap in his mind was appalling. 'It's a neat gimmick, but I don't believe it's going to solve our problems if we get a mass strike. You can't line everybody up and flash one of those things in front of his face before he gets away.'

'There are other applications of the same principle.'

Warner smiled without humor. 'But you are right. It will not solve the problem of getting the production we need.

'It is all very difficult. Dealing with Earthmen is very difficult. You have an imagination, and an inquisitiveness which we have seldom encountered elsewhere. These are wonderful qualities for the young and growing planet, but they make our dealings with you extremely difficult.'

He turned to Ruth. 'Do you see any answer to this problem that they suspect is beginning to exist?'

'If I had known the true nature of your work from the beginning,' said Ruth, 'I would have done many things differently. It will take days of work to see how serious the situation really is. I suspect what the final solution may be, however, and I need not tell you now how drastic it appears.'

16

It was April when Jorgasnovara turned the Llannan properties over to Cal's supervision. In June, Cal and Ruth were married, and Jorgasnovara returned for his promised instruction tour of all Llannan properties on Earth.

Cal and Ruth laid their plans for the trip to do double duty as a honeymoon as well as a technical orientation tour. But the strain of the responsibilities toward the Llannan Council and toward Earth itself were too great to permit conventional honeymoon gaiety.

Only gradually did the darkness of the shadow under which they had agreed to live become apparent.

As Cal sweated over the delicate problems of the secrecy of the Peace Engineers there continued to unfold vast areas of knowledge which he knew his own people would not encounter for many decades, or even centuries. He felt almost a sense of guilt at possession of the great treasure of knowledge, and at the same time an overwhelming gratitude that it was his good fortune to possess it.

But the purpose of that possession still rankled in his mind. He accepted the righteousness of the Llannan cause; he accepted himself as a warrior mercenary. Only now, however, was there a full awareness of the extent to which he had committed not only himself, but all mankind.

He had not understood this at first. Not until he stood night after night at the great loading docks watching the ships of the Llanna carrying away into space the materials and substance of Earth itself.

The science and technology that had created those instruments belonged to the Llanna, but the substance and the labor belonged to Earth. There was significance in this. The materials that were being hurled into the great conflict were, in a sense, the possession and property of each man of Earth. By dedicating them to the Llannan cause, Cal Meacham knew that he had in effect dedicated each man of Earth to that same cause.

Jorgasnovara came at the end of June, after Cal and Ruth had been married for two weeks. To them, the Engineer looked more tired than before he left, as if his vacation had been devoted to even heavier duties. His massive hands trembled almost visibly as he sat across from them in his office at the plant.

'We've got to have more interocitors,' he said. 'There are only a dozen worlds on which these instruments can be effectively produced, and Earth is one of the best of these. Production has got to double and triple here, and we've got to find new worlds where they can be made.'

'It can't be done here,' said Cal. 'Not by simply expanding the size of the productive facilities we already have.'

Then he told Jorgasnovara about the labor unrest.

'You've got to solve that problem,' said the Llannan. 'That's your job. That's the thing you have agreed to do.'

'Then you will have to let us do it in our own way. Increasing the size of this plant is not the way.'

'What is the way?' Jorgasnovara demanded.

'We've figured out what we think is a solution. I'll let Ruth tell it.'

'Decentralization. Cybernetic control – those are the answers,' said Ruth. 'The only ones we can see now.'

Jorgasnovara shook his head. 'It has taken too long to

build this up here. We haven't time. And the plants would not be any less conspicuous if they were operated by negligible manpower.'

'We would not be threatened by strikes,' said Cal, 'which is our immediate problem. That will cost us more time than if we broke up the plant into scattered units. If we did that, we could eventually become as big as you like, but this plant is impossible to operate under the secrecy requirements you have. The question of strike is the thing that will defeat it.'

The Llannan Engineer shook his head. 'That's among the most curious customs I have found on Earth. I have never found another planet where it operates. Must it be allowed to run its course? Is there no way of preventing it?'

'I have done what I can, but your requirements place too much strain on our peculiar human nature. It's like a reactor building to critical mass.'

'Can you explain why?'

'It's fairly simple,' Cal said. 'Out of necessity a man assigns control of his life to whatever employment he is engaged in. Nine times out of ten it is not the thing he would be doing if he had free choice. When he loses control of himself in such a manner anger builds up. When the accumulated anger of a mass of workmen reaches its critical peak it is expressed. They strike.

'After such a period of dramatization, the anger subsides, they go back to work, and the cycle begins building again. It's virtually inevitable unless suppression of the individual is practised to the point where they cannot strike.

'During most of the history of Earth such suppression has been the case. Only recently has it become possible to strike, and on the whole it is probably a healthy thing – but not conducive to high interocitor production. Where it is unknown, I would guess that there is either no need to work, or complete suppression.'

'Do you think it safe to take the tour at this time?' said Jorgasnovara. 'Would it be better to stay here and attend to these matters?'

'I've got to become acquainted with the other plants if I'm going to administer them. I think we should leave at once, and gamble on getting back and reaching a solution before it explodes – which it will do if we cannot persuade you to permit drastic changes.'

They left by commercial airline the same afternoon in order to avoid tying up a Llannan ship needed in more urgent freight service.

They rushed across the desert, the great wheatlands, and above the smoke-crowned industrial centers. It was all the same and yet so different. No one would suspect it was part of the arsenal of the Guarra-Llannan struggle. It gave Cal a chill as he thought of it. Their efforts were so puny. But multiplied by tens of thousands of other worlds similarly engaged, perhaps it was not so.

On the way to Gander they stopped at a Canadian paper mill. A tiny place which turned out a few tons a day of the special kind of paper used in the memory imprinting textbooks of the Llanna.

In England they visited a textile mill. The purpose of its product was incomprehensible to Cal. Jorgasnovara gave up trying to explain it to him. In France, they saw a die making shop where skilled craftsmen turned out structures like weird, surrealistic sculpture. Jorgasnovara explained that they were actually three dimensional projections of certain intricate equations and were used as control templates in some of the war computers of the Llannan Council.

Swiss instrument shops. Italian ceramic factories. They

128

visited a score of such where workmen busily turned out devices whose purposes were unknown to them. Cal felt stunned by the actual contact with the far-flung enterprise he had agreed to administer. For the first time, he began to understand its vastness, even on Earth.

All the places they saw were comparatively small shops, each one supervised by a Llannan technologist, whom Jorgasnovara wanted to replace as quickly as possible. None of the plants was of the scope of the interocitor plant in Phoenix.

Cal and Ruth were startled when the Llannan set the course of their tour for the African coast. But there they found a small settlement of native craftsmen skillfully turning objects in ivory. The purpose of these, too, was inexplicable to the Earth mind.

And then from Dakar they took a plane to Rio. They were in Peru, at the shops where skilled gold- and silver-smiths hammered intricate patterns in the precious metals, and Cal and Ruth wondered why it couldn't have been done a thousand times more efficiently by machine shop and assembly line methods.

There, word from Ole caught up with them. The interocitor plant was closed down. The union had struck.

'This is it,' said Cal, as he handed the radio message to Jorgasnovara. 'I was wrong. We should have stayed. We'll have to catch the next plane.'

Jorgasnovara glanced somberly at the message. 'Have you an immediate plan?'

'We've told you what we advise. Why didn't you follow the plan of the small European plants when you built the American one?' he said. 'Most of them are secure. You won't have trouble there.'

'I don't see the difference. We couldn't build them alike. Interocitor production is a big thing. It demands an enormous factory. To break it up would have seemed senseless. Just why are the European plants better?'

'Simply because they're smaller,' said Cal. 'Somewhere there must be a natural limit of size in which the secrecy of these projects can be maintained. I don't know what that limit may be. Perhaps we can find it mathematically. It's what we've got to do.

'We must manufacture parts in decentralized locations, ship them to one assembly plant controlled cybernetically by a very few employees on the engineer level.'

Jorgasnovara continued to shake his head. 'No. It would mean starting the entire project over again. We haven't the time for that in this critical stage.'

On arriving in Phoenix, they found the pattern of the strike was a familiar one. Ole had been forced to discharge an obviously incompetent assembler. The union seized upon this opportunity they had long awaited.

The same afternoon they arrived, they met with the union representatives in Cal's office. Cushman, the shop steward, was a squat, defiant little man who reminded Cal very much of a bantam rooster. Biggers, the union negotiator, on the other hand, was tall and suave, and needed only a Homburg to complete his diplomatic bearing.

'You've got to put Smithers back on,' said Cushman bluntly as he sat down across the desk from Cal, 'or we don't go back. That's final.'

'I understand the complaint,' said Cal, 'was that Smithers was unable to perform the assembly operation assigned to him. Our contract with your union clearly states that the required level of competence shall exist in an employee or he shall not be retained.'

'You switched jobs on Smithers,' said Cushman. 'He was doing all right as a screw and nut man which was what you hired him for. Then you switched him to soldering operations. They've been laying for him for weeks at the plant. I've seen it. When they couldn't get anything else on him, his assignment was switched. We won't stand for it.'

Cal sighed. 'How about this, Ole?'

Ole shrugged and spread his hands in resignation. 'We changed the fastening operation on a sub-assembly and soldering lugs were substituted for previous nut and bolt fastenings. Smithers' old assembly operation never existed. We assigned him the new one. He couldn't tell a soldering iron from a burned out cigar stub. He held up the entire assembly line. We had to let him go.'

'It was a deliberate trick,' said Cushman. 'We won't stand for it, I tell you. We're here to defend the rights of this boy, and we don't go back to work until he's back on.'

Biggers cleared his throat lightly and spoke for the first time. 'It would certainly seem, gentlemen, that some sort of compromise could be reached. It may well be that the – ah – intellectual qualifications of Mr Smithers are somewhat limited. That, I think, however, should not prevent him from achieving full and honest employment. There must be numerous menial tasks which he could adequately perform.'

'They are already being performed,' snapped Cal. 'Our janitorial force is filled with union men, and we have no position with any standard of competency lower than that of an assembler. If Smithers can't handle a soldering iron he'd better find a location somewhere on the end of a shovel.'

'Then it appears that we shall have to resort to – ah – mediation,' said Biggers. 'And, of course, in the meantime we shall be obliged to picket.'

Cal looked steadily at the two men without speaking. He wondered what would happen if he told them about the conflict being fought across a few hundred million light years of space. How would they react to the information that the interocitors were contributing to that cosmic struggle?

They wouldn't understand it, of course. They'd laugh in his face. And it was obvious that the Llanna had been wise in one regard, not coming into the open and inviting Earth to contribute.

There were too many little fires to be kept burning here. Ones like this. He wondered what parallel might exist between the little struggle here and the bigger one out in space. Was life so constituted that its common denominator from one end of eternity to the other was to strive with other life?

'Picket all you like,' said Cal. 'We may not open the plant again at all.'

Jorgasnovara was not at the conference, considering it beyond the scope of his own ability to comprehend the wrangle over labor details. While Ruth, Ole, and Dr Warner remained to try working out some basis for mediation, Cal went to report personally to Jorgasnovara.

He found the Engineer seated at his desk, his head bowed in his hands. The interocitor at the side of the room was activated, but its screen was blank.

He looked up slowly as Cal entered. The deep set eyes gave a momentary frightening impression of being burned out. Then he rubbed them vigorously and straightened in the chair.

'I'm glad you came,' he said. 'I've just talked with our moon base.'

'What is it?'

Jorgasnovara hesitated, glancing towards the huge rolls of star charts that could be unfolded against one wall. 'I hardly know how to tell you this,' he said slowly. 'I hadn't supposed that it would happen.'

He walked over to the wall and unrolled one of the great charts, spreading it to cover the entire wall and fastening it at the opposite corner.

His finger traced along a thick red line that ran in a jagged diagonal across the chart. 'This is a picture of a billion light years of space. Here is the present battle line. The report I have just received indicates that the entire lower quarter of the line has collapsed.'

With colored chalk he drew a new line to show the change. 'Here,' he said. 'Here is your galaxy.'

Cal's breath sucked in. He stared at the little white dot almost at the bottom of the chart, and at the jagged red line that was like a trail of blood across it.

'We had not foreseen this development,' said Jorgasnovara. 'The entire effort of the enemy has been on the opposite end of the line. You must understand that this is not merely a line but represents a plane in three dimensional space. The whole Guarra effort has been to extend that plane upward on the chart. Now that effort has been shifted and he is sweeping inward on the lower end. Sweeping toward this galaxy in which you Earthmen live.'

17

'What does it mean for Earth?' said Cal in a tight voice. 'Can the Llannan Council hold that line?'

'I think so. We're shifting forces to meet the threat. Somehow we should have been able to predict this. You can't fight a war you can't predict – ' His head shook in dismay.

Cal ignored the question that surged in his mind – how could you predict war at all? He was staring again at the narrow gap between the battle line and his own galaxy.

'The line is important,' Jorgasnovara went on. 'The Guarra are only a few hundred light years from our largest engine factory. We cannot permit such a position to fall.'

He rolled the chart back again. 'But it is serious,' he said. 'Very serious. Every production center has to be called upon to make increased output. I tell you this not to frighten you with a threat to Earth – which I think is remote as ever – but to impress upon you the urgency of our needs.

'Tell me. What was the solution arrived at with the union?'

'There was no solution,' said Cal. 'And there can't be. We've got to change our program regardless of how urgent the need for production is. As a matter of fact, urgency is all the more reason for changing.'

Jorgasnovara turned away and faced the window toward the main plant building. Cal could see his head was moving slowly in a negative gesture.

'No,' the Llannan said, 'I will not permit that to be

done in spite of what has happened. There have to be other answers. In a sense, our work here is expendable. If it becomes impossible to hold the present battle line in some future time we can always retreat and find another civilization to do the work we have chosen yours to do.

'But at this precise moment in time continued production is urgent. We will continue it along present lines until it collapses of its own weight – if that is inevitable.

'Elsewhere, other Engineers will already be setting up new plants on new worlds in case of our withdrawal here. You will please go ahead as the program has been outlined.'

Expendable.

The word chilled Cal. He thought of green jungle islands during the war, native villages smashed and people driven aside only to be ignored in pain and misery when the tide of battle swept past.

One thing Jorgasnovara had never understood was the tragic magnitude of the decision that had changed Cal Meacham from a pacifist to a war maker, but if that decision could not be recognized for what it was by the Llannan it had better not have been made.

Cal faced Jorgasnovara, his voice shaking as he spoke. 'I'll manage the project in the manner I consider necessary, or not at all. I know my own people, and what they will do.'

For a moment the two stood looking silently at each other. Cal felt an intimation of the terrible power latent behind the Engineer's eyes, and wondered if that power were going to be turned against him.

Jorgasnovara shifted his weight. He stepped toward Cal. 'We can compromise,' he said gently. 'I chose you because I knew you had the strength and the ability to tell us what we need to know. We will begin the process of building up the diffused assembly centers as you have suggested, but let us not close down here until they are completed and in operation. Do you think that will be satisfactory?'

'It won't be. Every minute that this plant is in operation we are running risks of exposure.'

'We'll take it. In the meantime, the other half of the program will get under way.'

'And you will have to get some new boys to take over when Ruth and Ole and I are doing a ten year stretch for un-American activities.'

'I don't understand.'

'Skip it. I've got to run down with my hat in my hand and ask the union boys to please go back to their jobs.'

It was late, and he was not able to find Biggers or Cushman that day. He thought afterwards that he might have been able to do it if he had not given way to his feelings of frustration in the face of Jorgasnovara's conflicting demands. He should have exerted himself to run them down, to get the plant in operation to avoid losing a day's production.

But he did not.

At four o'clock the next morning he was awakened by a call from the plant. It was Peterson, the temporary watchman, coming on at change of shifts. There was the sound of tears and terror in his voice.

'They wrecked the place, Mr Meacham,' he bawled. 'They wrecked the place!'

'What are you talking about?'

'The strikers! They wrecked the place. George must have been drugged. He didn't hear a thing.'

Cal's mind seemed to wait in a condition of stasis while his body went through the mechanical motions of donning his clothes.

Maybe it's the way it should be, he thought. We'll let

them get away with it. We'll let them go, and they'll be too scared to talk. And Jorgasnovara will have to do things the right way.

He called Ole, who met him and Ruth at the main gate.

When they arrived, there was no one there except the custodial employees, and the plant was mostly dark. He was glad for that. He wanted this quiet as yet.

Peterson, a conscientious old man, let them in at the side door. His hand trembled so greatly he could scarcely manipulate the lock.

'They may still be around the plant,' he said nervously. 'You shouldn't have come without the police, Mr Meacham.'

'I don't think they'll do us any harm,' said Cal. 'And they probably beat it long ago. You keep watch at the door. Don't let anyone else in until I give the word. We'll take a look.'

The three passed on into the corridor leading to the main assembly room. The extent of the damage was obvious. It was not merely the overturning of furniture and scattering of parts that could have been restored with comparative ease. At each station along the assembly line all valuable and some almost irreplaceable metering and test equipment had been methodically smashed.

Cal marched at a slow pace the full length of the assembly line, Ruth at his side. Ole paused here and there, poking into the shards of shattered equipment, then hurrying to catch up with Cal and Ruth, stopping once more to investigate another station of disaster like a frightened ant whose tunnels have been destroyed by a boy with a stick.

In an adjoining wing of the building they examined the screen rooms of the test department. Here the damage was even greater. The complex instruments required to make final tests of the interocitor assemblies were smashed beyond repair.

'You could hardly ask for a more thorough job,' said Cal bitterly. 'We ought to invite all the strikers through here to take a look. Let them have a piece for a souvenir. It ought to make them feel very good.'

'Don't blame the union,' said Ruth. 'They don't support this kind of thing. It's the crackpot morons who get in that are responsible for this.'

'The union is responsible!' said Cal. 'It's responsible because it admits and upholds and goes on strike on behalf of the crackpots and morons. Each individual member of the organization is responsible for this as long as he votes and strikes in support of a sub-normal moron we need to remove in order to run a factory. There's no way on Earth they can escape that responsibility.'

Ole joined them abruptly. 'What do you suppose Jorgasnovara will do now? Do you think he'll make us rebuild this place or go ahead with the dispersal?'

'It would be insane to rebuild here,' said Cal. 'If he insists on that I'm through. The raw part of this whole deal is that we can't publicly or legally lay the blame on the union. All we can do is take it. If we tried to sue them for damages that would blow the whole enterprise wide open.

'The only satisfaction possible would be the flattening of Biggers' nose, but probably we'd better not allow ourselves even that small pleasure. At least I think we have a club we can hold over the union's head that may be even better than a punch in the nose.'

He went into the office and put in a call for Biggers and Cushman. They showed up within a half hour and Cal led them without warning into the assembly room.

The two union men stared with mouths agape, and Biggers paled so genuinely that Cal was almost disturbed about their guilt until he realized that these two were professionals. Undoubtedly they had expected this call and were prepared to act their parts.

'It's a good job your goon squad did,' he said. 'So good that this plant simply isn't going to run any more.'

'Our boys never done nothing like this!' Cushman said. 'What do you think we are – a bunch of lousy Red saboteurs? You try to hang this one on us, and we'll really show you what we can do. As a matter of fact, I'll bet you arranged this yourself just to lay it on the union.'

Biggers turned more calmly to Cal. 'I assure you, Mr Meacham, our men had nothing to do with the affair. I am sure that, in view of the high priority secrecy of your project, there are other explanations. Communist sabotage, as my companion suggested, is the most likely. We shall do all we can to assist you in running down the culprits.'

'Look,' said Cal. 'We know who did this and we know why it was done. We're taking this plant out of production completely and making substitute assembly by cybernetic techniques. That means we don't intend to have anything to do with your union now or ever. If you try to molest or organize one of our plants again a complete record of this sabotage and a suit for full damages will be thrown into court.

'We'd do it now, except that it would be of no value to us except as an act of revenge, and we are not interested in that. You could not repay the monetary damage, and nothing would be accomplished by trying to avenge ourselves on you. What we do have is a good thick club, and we'll let you have it if your union ever approaches one of our plants again.'

'We won't stand for it,' said Biggers. 'You can't smear our record that way. We want it cleared – now! This is blackmail.'

139

Ole grunted harshly and swept a hand over the wreckage. 'Blackmail, the man says!'

Biggers and Cushman left without further argument, but with a promise to see Cal later.

'We'll never see those birds again,' Cal prophesied. 'I'll bet they're glad to get off so easy.'

'I don't think they did it,' said Ruth quietly. 'I think they were honestly as shocked as we were when they came in.'

'I suppose you're going to tell me now that it's some subtle Llannan scheme of Jorgasnovara's,' Cal snapped irritably.

'No, I just don't think the union did. I've studied human beings long enough to know genuine surprise when I see it. I don't know who did this, but we may be very greatly surprised when we find out.'

Jorgasnovara expected to leave within a short time, and was preparing his office for his final departure when Cal entered with news of the disaster.

'The plant's useless,' he said. 'There's no point at all in rebuilding here. I told the union that we would not reopen.'

Jorgasnovara sat unmoving. His massive arms spread the width of the broad desk clenching each side with white knuckled hands.

'It isn't possible, is it,' he said slowly, 'that you had something to do with the arrangement of this in order to assure the carrying out of your program rather than mine?'

Cal continued to look at him without changing expression or offering to speak.

'I just wanted to make sure,' said Jorgasnovara. 'I don't understand Earthmen very well. This destruction – it's the work of an enemy, not of members of your own kind.'

'The enemy out there – ' Cal nodded to the war charts, ' – that is no different. Life fighting life – it's no more understandable than this stupid act of the union.'

'Perhaps you're right.' Jorgasnovara rose. 'I can't give you an immediate answer. I'll have to consult with my superiors for further instructions. Let me call you later in the day.'

Cal nodded agreement and left the offices. Suddenly, outside the door, he realized that there was nowhere to go. There was no factory to be run. There were no interocitors to be made.

He returned to his own office and called Ruth and Ole. 'School's out, kids,' he said. 'Let's make it a holiday.'

It was an insane thing, but they were all just a little insane, he thought. You don't work and sleep with an intergalactic conflict and remain entirely sane.

They gathered picnic things and set out along one of the desert roads. Recent spring rains had sent long dormant flowers bursting from the desert floor. The wasteland was a garden as far as they could see.

At the edge of a low hill they gathered dry cactus and added packing case lumber they had brought from the plant. Within a few minutes the comforting sizzle of frying steaks merged with the desert silence. Ruth sat on a rock, her knees drawn up.

'It would be easy to forget all about Jorgasnovara, and all his Llannan Council now,' she said.

'Are you suggesting we do that?' said Ole.

'I don't know whether I am or not. It's just that there's no end to it. Anything else that people do has a logical and reasonable end either in their own lifetime or they can pass it on to their children, but this – There's nothing to end it, and no goal to pass on with assurance of its being achieved. Everything connected with it seems so purposeless and endless.'

'Anything connected with war,' said Cal, 'is always useless except at the very moment you are defending your own life. You never know quite what it's all about until that moment comes. And when it does, you wish you could go back a year, a decade, a century maybe and kill not merely the one who attacks you but the blunderers who brought you to that moment.'

'That sounds a lot different from the Cal Meacham of some months ago,' said Ole.

Cal shook his head. 'No. It's the same one. I knew such moments during the war. I'm just convinced that I've been brought to such a moment again, and I wish with all my heart that I could go back a century or a millennium and face the ones who have brought it.'

At that moment they were interrupted by the alarm of the portable set in the car. It was Jorgasnovara.

'Please return to my office as soon as possible,' he said. 'I have contacted the Planning Committee for Earth. They have given a decision on the present matter. In addition, they wish to know what your feelings are regarding the possibility of leaving Earth and taking up residence in the same work on a similar planet in another solar system.'

18

The three of them were almost mute on the trip back to the plant. It was not until they were again in the office that Ruth burst out, 'Another planet! Why?'

'There's nothing definite yet,' said Jorgasnovara. 'But the Committee is seriously considering the possibility of transferring the whole project to a more suitable location in case of necessity.

'I have recommended to them that if such should be necessary you three would be very desirable to continue with the project, if you would consider it.'

'You can't ask for an answer to that,' said Cal, 'until the time comes absolutely and definitely. Why should they consider removal of operations from Earth, anyway?'

'The Committee is disturbed by this strike situation. It is something they never anticipated. They understood the customs of your people, but it was supposed that your administration could see that such an emergency did not arise, particularly since you are authorized for unlimited use of funds, and that appeared to be the cause of strikes.'

Cal knew that his face was deepening in color and he tried to keep his breath from coming faster in rage. 'I've told you before that money is the last thing that men strike for. And I warned you that it was coming long before it did. My only error was in estimating the time. But if my warnings had been given attention, we might have been able to prevent the whole thing.

'But what about the program now? Are we to go ahead?'

Jorgasnovara shook his head. 'The Committee has

reversed my decision to build decentralized plants to run parallel to this one. You might suppose that they would abandon this one completely. The answer is no.

'They demand restoration of the present plant. Their computers show this can be done in less than sixty percent of the time required to get your plan for dispersed centers into operation.'

'Then I refuse to have any more to do with it,' flared Cal. 'I was supposed to administer this program, and it turns out that the Llannan Council believes it knows more about Earthmen than we do ourselves. You see the results! They can continue running it.'

He stalked out of the office and returned to his own. There was for a moment a tremendous sense of freedom that he had not known since first hearing of the Peace Engineers. He gave a short laugh of disgust as he thought of the starry-eyed wonder with which they had fished him in. Supermen – who didn't have sense enough to come in out of the rain.

But suddenly he stopped laughing. That was right. They *were* supermen, from a technological standpoint. And they *didn't* know enough to come in out of the rain, from a psychological standpoint. Why, he wondered? What was lacking that made them unable to understand what was necessary in dealing properly with Earthmen? The organization had been around for a couple of hundred years, Jorgasnovara said. And they had learned so little!

He tried to make the first move to gather his papers and personal belongings, but he continued to sit there, his hands motionless on the desk top as he considered the imponderable behavior of the Llanna.

How did the Llannan Council manage to keep tens of thousands of manufacturing plants in line with such tactics as these? He didn't know, but maybe it was important to find out – to find out this and a good number of other things about the Llanna.

He glanced down at the drawers which he ought to be emptying. He wasn't going to empty them, he thought. The Llannan Council actually needed much more help than he had supposed – more than they even realized themselves! And he had committed himself to their aid as long as the Guarra legions were rampant in the depths of space.

At that moment the door opened and Ruth walked in. 'Over your mad?' she said casually.

Cal permitted a wry grin. 'Yeah, I guess so. What did he say?'

'He was pretty upset, but I told him you didn't mean it. I was surprised at you. I thought you had discovered a long time ago that there was no walking out on this.'

'I just discovered it now.'

'Good. Then we won't have any more nonsense like this. Jorgasnovara says that a shipment of replacement equipment for the plant will be on its way from the sub-storage base serving this area. It should be ready for the beginning of installation tomorrow.'

He spent the remainder of the day with Ole supervising the removal of debris and making ready for re-installation. Contacting the union, he re-established relations with them – to the point of backing down on the accusations he had made.

This enabled him to get a few key men back on the job that afternoon.

Standard Earth equipment was ordered by wire and flown in from distant parts of the country. Most of these arrived by the next morning. The Llannan ship docked during the night and deposited its load of emergency replacement parts so that by the following afternoon the plant was stocked with many of the necessary components to restore operation.

When quitting time came that day, Ruth was with Cal surveying the stacks of crates and the long assembly lines now cleared of wreckage and waiting for installation of the complex test and assembly tools.

'Suppose it happens again,' said Ruth quietly.

Cal jerked his head to look at her. 'Suppose what happens again? You think those crazy union goons would be dumb enough to break in here again?'

'So you still think it was the union?'

'Who else?'

'I don't know. All I know is the way Biggers and Cushman looked when they first saw the wreckage. They understood who would get the blame.'

'You bet they did!'

'But if the union didn't do it, it's liable to happen again.' She glanced at the stacks of crates whose value was undetermined in Earth figures, but which they knew were worth more than a couple of million dollars at best.

'It might even happen tonight with all this brand new equipment standing around inviting trouble.'

'There'll be guards, as usual.'

'Let's you and I stand watch in the plant tonight,' said Ruth, 'to guard the guards, as it were.'

'That's the craziest idea I've heard of since I first met an interocitor,' said Cal.

'Just for the heck of it, huh?'

He spread his hands helplessly.

'I'll make some sandwiches and sneak them into the office in a brief-case and we'll just stay after hours. Set up an interocitor somewhere in the plant so that it can be energized and we can pick up the thoughts of whoever is down there.'

'It should be highly entertaining to learn what mice think about in the middle of the night,' said Cal.

With grumbling reluctance he agreed to humor Ruth and spend the night in the plant. He prepared to do some work at his desk until Ruth reminded him that they shouldn't show a light. Then he reclined full length on his back on the carpeted floor and stared up into the blackness of the ceiling shadows.

Ruth sat by the window. The interocitor headpiece partially covered her ears.

'I wish I knew what the devil you expect to find,' Cal muttered repeatedly.

'I wish I did, too.'

It was futile trying to get any other kind of answer out of her. Cal shut his eyes while he worried over the problem of how to get the dispersed facilities constructed over the heads of the Llanna.

As the hours passed, Ruth glanced repeatedly at the dial of her watch which glowed faintly in the dim light of a waning moon. She wondered if it had been a fool's hunch, after all. There was no reason to believe the sabotage would be repeated on this particular night. But there were other nights, she thought philosophically –

Of course, she would have to do any further watching alone. Cal would stand for no more nonsense of this kind. But she felt certain the attack would come again, and when it did they ought to be prepared to find the source of it.

It was just after midnight when the first alien whispering touched her senses. She had to stop an instant and think what it was that caught her attention.

'Cal,' she whispered. 'Cal!'

'Huh? Yeah – what is it?' He yawned in audible sleepiness.

'Cal – there aren't any ships due from the moon tonight, are there?'

'No. They brought everything belonging to this batch in the shipment last night. Why?'

'I just saw a shadow out there. It passed over us. Just a little shadow.'

'Probably some fool nightowl looking for the airport,' he muttered in disgust. 'Let's go home and go to bed, Ruth. We've got work to do tomorrow.'

'No, wait. Did you hear that?'

He sat up sharply and jumped to his feet, suddenly wide awake and alert. There had been just the faintest tremor pass through the building. Something so far below the threshold of sound that it was totally inaudible. There had been a distant impact that affected some deep sense besides that of hearing.

'It landed on the roof,' whispered Ruth. 'We can get up there if we hurry, and see who gets out.'

Cal's hand stopped her impulsive flight toward the door. 'This doesn't make sense. I don't think anybody landed on the roof.'

But he knew it wasn't true.

'Let's try the interocitor.' He stepped to the controls that Ruth had temporarily abandoned. He energized the instrument he had left down in the plant near the assembly lines.

Standing in the darkness with the headpieces on, they slowly became aware of faint impulses and images like some strange, other-world thoughts. Ruth was suddenly trembling as if hit by an emotional blast she could not withstand. Cal felt the back of his neck turn cold. He swore softly.

'Cal, what is it?' Ruth murmured.

'What kind of men are they?'

'That's it! They're not men – '

148

They attuned their thoughts to the flowing mental waves that came through the interocitor, but there was nothing recognizable in terms of human words or ideas. It was a flowing stream of sheer evil.

Ruth threw off the headpiece. 'I can't stand that anymore. What are we going to do, Cal?'

He turned up the illumination of the instrument, but there were only shapeless shadows visible in the darkened plant. Abruptly there was a faint crunching sound followed by the clatter of metal and glass.

'They're smashing things,' said Ruth. 'But how can they keep the noise so muffled?'

'I don't know. You stay here. I'm going to try to make it down to the watchman's locker. Mac has a gun around there somewhere. If I'm not back in twenty minutes call Ole to bring help.'

'No, I'm going with you.'

'You stay here!' Cal ordered with sudden hardness in his voice. 'This is no two-bit movie drama. We've got to find out who they are, and I need your help up here.'

In darkness, Cal moved into the corridor. He felt his way along the wall until he reached the stairway leading to the main assembly floor below. Moving down slowly he could hear more plainly the sounds of destruction as cases were ripped open and their contents smashed.

Then he was aware of an odor that filled him with sudden nausea. He stifled a sudden choking agony in his throat. He grabbed a handkerchief and wadded it against his nose, cautiously drawing short breaths through it.

The smell was like that of some age-old jungle where slimy things crept and crawled in darkness. He knew of no source within the plant that could have released such a gas upon being smashed. Momentarily, he wondered if the saboteurs had released some anesthetic to protect themselves while they worked. But it didn't have that kind of effect. It was merely nauseating.

Holding his breath for a large part of the time and breathing cautiously, he gained a degree of conditioning towards the odor. At last he reached the watchman's closet. He wondered what had become of the men on duty, if the invaders had killed them –

He did not think the union would stoop to murder. But was he sure now that these were union goons? They weren't, he told himself. He didn't know who or what they were, but they represented nothing that he had ever experienced before in his life.

He found the gun he was looking for and checked it by touch. He wet his handkerchief in the washbowl in the small room and applied it again to his nose as he moved back toward the assembly room. He carried a large flashlight in one coat pocket and the gun in the other, moving slowly along by finger touch.

The noise of demolition increased. He moved forward even more cautiously as he approached it, trying to orient the sound by ear. Then he had it placed.

They were working in one of the screen rooms where a few pieces had been uncrated and tentatively set up. Not a ray of light shone anywhere. They were working somehow in complete darkness, as if they could see without light.

But that was fantastic. Yet if it were true, the darkness was no protection at all to him –

He tried to keep behind the protection of the assembly line storage cabinets, waiting for the sound of the saboteurs to emerge from the screen room. He had grown accustomed to the nauseous odor so that he could abandon the handkerchief now as long as he confined his breath to short intakes.

With one hand he held the flashlight in front of him and

the gun in the other. A tremor of apprehension went through him as a sound of shuffling, dragging feet came near the door and passed out of the screen room. He flicked the switch on the light.

He knew he must have screamed aloud at the sight. Two figures faced him, clad in suits that completely covered them from head to foot. The upper half was semi-transparent, and through the covering he could see grotesque features that he knew belonged nowhere upon Earth.

They were green and minutely scaly and spoke of alien swamp lands. Tiny puffs of greenish atmosphere with the overpowering odor exuded from the vents in the suits.

Cal raised the gun to fire. He watched it come up as if observing a distant, slow motion film. He saw his finger begin to squeeze the trigger. In the instant of doing so, a crushing blow smashed against his skull from behind.

His body twisted half around and he collapsed against the floor. His last vision was of the two alien creatures looking with a kind of unbelievable satisfaction beyond him to one who stood behind.

19

The light made a blinding sheet of the green walls that surrounded him. He closed his eyes against its hurt. He guessed vaguely that he was in the single hospital room of the plant dispensary.

The people around him would be Ruth and Ole and Jorgasnovara. Maybe Doc Howard and one of the nurses, but he was too tired to open his eyes again to make sure.

He felt cool hands touching his own and resting against his cheek. That would be Ruth. He smiled a little in appreciation of her presence.

'He's coming around now,' he heard someone say. It was Doc Howard, all right. 'We'd better go out now, and leave him alone.'

Cal opened his eyes again and moved a hand.

'No,' he murmured. 'No.'

Ruth glanced at the Doctor, who shrugged permission and left her with Cal. Ole and Jorgasnovara remained for a moment.

'What happened?' said Ole. 'Can you tell us what happened to you?'

What had happened? Cal thought dully. He'd given up the ideals he had once lived by because he became convinced he no longer lived in a world where they applied. Now he was face to face with the thing he had undertaken to combat. He turned to Jorgasnovara, his lips silent, but his eyes seeking confirmation.

The Llannan Engineer nodded as if understanding Cal's unspoken question.

'Yes, they were Guarra agents,' he said. 'We should

have suspected from the first. The pattern has occurred elsewhere. What did they look like? Did you get to see?'

Reconstruct all your childhood nightmares, and then you'll know, Cal thought. He tried to picture to Jorgasnovara the moment of horror when he flashed his light on the scaly, suited creatures.

'Suoinard,' said Jorgasnovara. 'I don't understand why they were picked for this job. Other species among the Guarra are almost identical with Earthmen. Perhaps they are rather desperate to accomplish this particular piece of work.'

'What work?' said Cal. 'What are they doing?'

'Trying to destroy interocitor production. It's much easier to do it by sending a couple of agents for sabotage than it is to send a fleet to devastate an entire planet.'

The words of the Llannan seemed to roll against the walls of the room and echo thunderously in his ears. He tried to shut out the sound and closed his eyes against the light that was too bright again.

He hadn't faced the risk before. He had just imagined that he had. The risk of putting himself and all mankind face to face with an enemy out of space, whose technology could wipe the planet clean of life.

'What will they do, now that we know about them?' said Cal. 'They got away, didn't they?'

'Yes – they got away. I don't know what they'll do next. Don't you worry about that. We'll talk about it when the time comes. For the next two or three days Ole and I will continue the work of rebuilding the assembly lines.'

They left in a little while, leaving him and Ruth alone. Ruth put her head against his chest, both of her hands clasping one of his.

'We should never have taken it on,' she murmured. 'It's too big for us. We are like the jungle islanders trying to fight with poisoned arrows against an enemy who has atomic bombs. If those arrows annoy the enemy enough he might blast the whole island out of existence.'

'There's no danger.' Cal patted her hand. 'The Llanna will see to it that the Guarra make no real threat to Earth. They promised that this would be so.'

But to him his voice sounded hollow as it echoed from the bare plaster walls.

'They haven't! The Guarra are here – and look what they've done to you,' cried Ruth. 'Cal, don't you know who it was that struck you?'

'One of the Guarra, of course! There must have been at least three of them. I thought they were all in the screen room, but one must have been waiting for me. They can probably see in the dark – by infra-red, I suppose.'

'Cal – I heard them talking through the interocitor. Not all of them were so alien as the ones you saw. I could understand the thoughts of one of them.'

He could feel the almost uncontrollable shaking of her body now, and raised her head so that he could look into her eyes. They were wide with terror.

'It was Ole, Cal – ! It was Ole Swenberg who struck you!'

Cal half raised his head from the pillow in spite of the pain.

'Ole! You're crazy – Ole and I have known each other since he went to college. How could he be guiding the Guarra agents?'

'He's not only their guide, he *is* a Guarra agent.' Ruth's voice was low and she glanced about the bare room as if fearful of being overheard. 'I know it's crazy, but I wasn't mistaken. I heard him.'

Cal's head sank back on the pillow wearily. 'You know

you're mistaken, Ruth. How can you insist on such a fantastic thing?'

'I don't know what it all means, but you've got to believe I'm right. Ole's just waiting for a chance to stab you in the back. He meant to kill you. He was disappointed that he didn't succeed. He'll try again.'

'The strain of all this has been more than you could take,' said Cal gently. 'You're believing the impossible. I lived with Ole for months. We swapped ties and shirts and girl friends at college. Go home and get some sleep and then come back and tell me it's a nightmare we've both been having.'

'It's a nightmare, but not the kind you have asleep. I'm not going to leave you. I'll sleep on the cot in the first aid room. I'm not going to give Ole a chance again.'

She kissed him quickly and fled from the room before he could protest. In a way he was glad. His throat felt too tired to answer. His head seemed to burn from hot fires somewhere deep within it. There was no use arguing with Ruth over this fantastic thing at this time. She would get over it when morning came.

But grey dawn was painful when it came. He was aware of little all that day. He knew that people came in to talk, but he was too tired to talk. His temperature was checked and he was fed, and Ruth sat by the bed and put her hand in his. And this brought back a nightmare where she said something about Ole trying to kill him. He wished he could wake up from it.

During the night he slept well, and on the following morning the nightmare was gone. He awoke with clear vision, and the fuzziness had gone out of his head. Some of the pain remained, but it didn't overshadow everything else now.

He struggled to sit up as dawn of the second morning lighted the room. His head spun and he had to hold it for a moment to dispel the feeling that it was entirely disconnected from his shoulders.

The feeling passed, and he was remembering. He had to see Jorgasnovara. He had to see Ole. He had to find out what was being done about the Guarra agents.

Ruth came in while he was getting his clothes out of the closet.

'Cal! You're not able to get up yet.'

'Both willing and able,' he said, tottering slightly as he sorted the clothes. 'Help me with these things.'

They ate breakfast from the meager supplies Ruth had brought to supply her through her own vigil. Cal called Jorgasnovara with word that he was coming over. The Llannan offered to come to him, but Cal insisted he was able to get up.

There was a strange silence about the plant and over the entire desert surroundings as Cal and Ruth walked to the office. There seemed no activity at all in the direction of restoration of the plant.

'It looks like the place is being allowed to die a natural death,' Cal muttered.

When they walked into the Engineer's office, Cal felt a sudden shock. Jorgasnovara's bony features seemed even more gaunt, verging on the cadaverous. He looked up from the papers scattered about the desk. There was no smile in the greeting he offered.

'I hope there will be no permanent results of this injury,' he said.

Cal slid into a chair. 'I'm okay. I want to know where we go from here. The place looks dead. What goes on?'

For a long time Jorgasnovara simply looked at them, his hands resting on the desk as if in complete resignation. He spoke finally.

'Nothing goes on. We're moving out.'

'Out?' Cal's face was blank. 'Where – ?'

'Out of Earth. Out of this solar system. Out of the galaxy.'

For a wild moment Cal had a fleeting vision of two green beings with inhuman expressions upon their faces.

'What do you mean? Tell me what this is all about!'

'Our intelligence reports,' said Jorgasnovara very slowly, 'show that the Guarra have shifted their line of offense and are moving rapidly towards this solar system with this planet as their specific objective.

'This is the direct result of the failure of their agents to maintain a steady pressure of sabotage upon our production of interocitors. I told you we had seen the pattern before and that they considered it economical warfare to stop the flow of supplies at their source.

'We were unable to predict, however – and the error is wholly ours – that the Guarra would move their line so far in order to attack this source if their sabotage program failed. But they have moved. Therefore, our entire line is moving back. Our personnel and all salvageable equipment are being transferred as rapidly as possible.'

'But the Guarra will invade Earth!' Ruth cried. 'You've drawn them here and you promised we'd be safe if we helped you. You've got to hold them back!'

The Engineer's face grew even whiter as he spoke again. 'This is the decision of the Llannan Council,' he said. 'It is the result of error in our computations. Believe me, I am sorry. If I had foreseen a thing like this I would have turned down this assignment. I would not have willingly brought this upon you.'

'You are sorry! Sorry that you have drawn us into a conflict we can't fight – and then turn your back upon us – !'

'Though I realize it is small comfort for the loss of your home planet,' said Jorgasnovara, 'I can offer you personal safety. You will be transferred immediately to one of the other worlds suitable for your habitation. My own home planet is one of these. I would welcome you there, though I would not be so stupid as to suppose I could ever compensate for the loss of your own world.'

Only dimly, it seemed to Cal later, did he hear Ruth's almost hysterical outburst and Jorgasnovara's repeated sympathy.

So this is where it had led to, he thought. He remembered the long gone day when he first saw the strange bead-like condensers that were the beginning of his aptitude test for Peace Engineers. He wanted to laugh now at that phrase, but there was not left in him either humor or bitterness enough to ridicule those tragic words.

When had it begun? There was no way of knowing. It had been inevitable from the beginning. He had wanted something better for himself, and for all sentient life in the universe. He had been no more than a fish acting on a simple stimulus-response mechanism. The Llanna had only to hold out the brightly colored lure, and he was hooked.

He thought again of Earth, the island Earth, which he had gambled as a base for Llannan activities. And he thought of all those other islands he had seen where striving armies had fought and blasted and left desolation.

'Why?' he asked at last, in the vacuum of silence that had fallen over them. 'Why have we been left alone?

'We agreed to assist in this because we thought it was good to support life in the whole universe, wherever it might be. We need not have engaged in the war, you told us. The Guarra would not have come. Now you tell us they will come and the Llanna will make no move in our defense. Why?'

Jorgasnovara spread his hands. 'I have told you my personal feeling. There is no answer to "why", really. Our war computers say that we should not defend at this point. That is the only answer I can give you. Your world is not a world to those machines. It is only a pinpoint in space.

'I can give you only another day to prepare to leave. By tomorrow night we must have evacuated all we intend to take from Earth. Please be reasonable in the amount of baggage you wish to take with you. You will be allowed an almost unlimited amount within the bounds of prudence. The ship will leave about midnight tomorrow.'

Ruth's eyes blazed. 'What makes you think we're going?' she demanded. 'Do you think we could ever live with ourselves knowing we had betrayed Earth and fled from the thing we had brought upon it? You have said you did not understand Earthmen. You have never spoken a truer statement. When your ship leaves, it will be without us!'

Jorgasnovara's head bowed. 'I had supposed that's the way it would be. I will not try to dissuade you, but if you change your mind let me know. You will be welcome to the very last moment.'

20

Ruth's eyes were on a distant vision, as if she were already seeing that death out of space. 'What will it be like?' she said. 'What will it be like for us here on Earth?'

'If there is no defense it will be as easy and as merciful as any death can be,' said Jorgasnovara. 'A fleet will circle the Earth, pushing a wave of fire ahead of it. There will be a terrible panic for a few hours and then it will be over. The Guarra are very efficient in this respect. We have seen it many times.'

'You said, if there were no defense,' said Cal questioningly.

The Engineer nodded. 'Any defense near an inhabited planet causes a prolonged agony due to the fields set up by the opposing forces which interact and produce inter-dimensional spatial strains.

'For this reason we have always tried to establish lines of defense that do not approach inhabited planets. If the Llanna were to defend Earth it would have to be done outside the galaxy.'

They left the room after the interview, and went out into the sunlight. The desert heat was oppressive already, a burning reminder of the Guarra doom.

Cal sought the shade at the side of the building as a wave of weakness swept over him.

'We'd better go home,' said Ruth, 'where you can lie down.'

He nodded absently, staring into the distance. He felt caught up in some eternal now of space and time. The world was covered with the dusty sunlight that had existed forever here on this desert. The buildings of the Llanna, new under their dust coating, the mountains beyond the city to the south – all of this was eternal in this moment.

He shifted his weight and started walking and his movement broke that eternal now as he had broken the destiny of all the Earth.

'Where are you going?' said Ruth.

'Ole. I forgot about Ole. We've got to tell him. Maybe he'll want to go with Jorgasnovara.'

'No!' cried Ruth. 'Don't go near him, please! Won't you believe what I learned about him – '

There was a feeling of dullness – almost of stupidity – in Cal's mind at the doubled burden, which he had almost forgotten, Ruth's accusation of Ole added to the Llannan desertion.

There was something tremendously important at stake in this. He was aware that in these final days there would be only one thing of importance, the trust and fellowship of his own kind. Ole was important to him. Ole's understanding and respect was important. Ruth's accusation irritated him beyond endurance. Rudely, he ignored her.

The housing project was somewhat deserted. Many of the people had gone away for a few days pending settlement of the strike. Here and there a few kids rode tricycles in the dust of the streets, and housewives hung washing in their back yards. And in his mind Cal had a vision of a wave of fire sweeping all of this into blackness and darkness forever – because of him.

Ole's car was in the driveway as they drove up to his place. Through the window they glimpsed him moving rapidly about inside.

'I wonder why he wasn't down to the plant this morning,' said Cal. 'Maybe Jorgasnovara has already told him.'

Then Ole was opening the door. Unfamiliar, tight lines

in his face shaped it like a mask. The sight of it was a shock to Cal.

Beyond, the room was littered and upset. Books and suitcases and papers cluttered the chairs and floor.

'You've heard?' said Cal.

Ole nodded. 'I'm getting out. You're going with Jorgas-novara, I suppose?'

'If it would do any good we would go along. This way, we haven't any right to.'

'I've got a right to!' snapped Ole. Then his tension eased and he spoke more normally. 'I thought you'd make that decision, but you've got to come along. Turn it around: what good is it staying behind? You can accomplish nothing by your deaths. Out there we'll have a chance again. We can join the Llannan forces and fight the Guarra as long as we live. That's all there is left to us, but we haven't the right to back down on *that*.'

'Revenge is no worthwhile purpose,' said Cal, 'if it's that and nothing more. With Earth gone, there's nothing for any of us. But you go ahead and do what you think best. I'm not trying to change your mind.'

Ole's eyes lowered. He put his hands in his pockets and scuffed a toe against the pile of the rug. He opened his mouth as if to say something and then shut it without speaking.

Ruth glanced about and took a step toward the kitchen door. 'It smells as if you have a can of something very badly spoiled out here,' she said lightly. But Cal could see that she was trembling. He had to get her out of here before she blurted out some stupid accusation about Ole.

'Refrigerator went haywire,' grunted Ole. 'It was off a couple of days. I haven't cleaned up everything yet.'

He turned to piles of books and journals and made a business of shuffling through them. Ruth moved on through the door to the kitchen.

Cal moved a step closer. He started to ask her to come on out and let Ole finish packing. Then he caught a whiff of the odor Ruth had mentioned. He almost held his breath to keep from inhaling it. To keep from recognizing the associations that poured upon him.

When he moved, his foot made a shuffle on the floor. Ole was faster. He whirled from the books with a gun in his hand.

Cal lurched forward then drew back stunned by the sight of the gun and Ole's distorted face.

'Don't warn her,' Ole said, nodding toward the kitchen. 'Call her back in here.'

Cal was prepared to shout to Ruth to run out the back door, but she was already back in the room facing them.

She screamed at the sight of the gun. 'I told you, Cal!'

'Over here together.' Ole gestured with the gun.

'Why?' said Cal evenly. 'Just who are you, Ole?'

'Does it make any difference now? If it does, you may know that I am Martolan, chief Guarra agent for Earth.'

'Aren't you the Ole Swenberg that went to Central Tech with me?'

'Sure,' Ole grinned maliciously. 'There has been no mysterious switching of personalities. My entire life has been devoted to evaluating and combating the Llannan program on Earth. We hoped that it would not be necessary to spend our forces in wiping out this civilization of yours because the Llanna had leeched on to it, but their program has gone too far. The actual crisis was our failure to stop interocitor production without resort to sabotage. I did all I could to discourage you; now you will have to suffer the consequences of my failure.'

He suddenly raised his voice and snapped a string of guttural sounds in some alien tongue. Immediately, the bedroom door opened behind them and out strode the

163

two creatures Cal had confronted in the plant. With them came the increase of nauseous exudate in the air.

'The boys are a little smelly,' said Ole wryly. 'I knew you'd recognize it the moment you stepped in. It was too much to hope that Ruth could get it passed off as spoiled food.'

'What are you going to do?' said Ruth thinly. 'What is to become of us?'

'I'm leaving. Our work is done. You know what I *ought* to do with you.' His hand tightened on the gun. 'I ought to make sure there is no further risk of your causing me trouble. But actually I can't see any way that you can.

'So I'm going to take just a little risk because I don't want either of you to miss the opportunity of witnessing and experiencing what you have brought to all of Earth by your meddling. I find it very curious that you refuse to go with Jorgasnovara, but I know your people well enough to know you will stand by that decision.

'In there, quickly.' He gestured once more with the gun in the direction of the bedroom.

'In the closet there. It's a stout door, and I don't think you'll be able to break through it for several hours, and if you don't break through at all it will be rather sad. You'll probably find there is air enough if you don't expend too much of it trying to break out.'

The room was filled with the sickening odor of the two aliens. Ruth gagged and struggled for a clean breath, but Ole pushed her on into the shallow closet. They heard the click of the lock. Ole's footsteps died away, leaving them in silence and darkness except for a narrow crack of light at the bottom of the door.

Ruth was crying now. Cal put his arms about her, but did not try to stop her sobbing. From the other parts of the house, there was the violent sound of Ole's departure, the hasty gathering of belongings and slamming of doors.

And then it was abruptly quiet. Ruth's low sobbing ceased and she stirred in Cal's arms.

'Thanks, darling,' she murmured. 'I'm sorry I let go – How are we going to get out of here? Can you break the door open?'

Cal patted her arm and released her. He moved to the door and leaned his shoulder hard against it.

'I think I could do it if there was room to get a good shove, but it's hopeless inside this closet. The Llanna didn't put up ordinary sub-division houses when they built this development. These doors are good and the locks are better.'

Ruth touched her foot along the bottom of the wall. 'This is plaster. Maybe it would be easier to break through that.'

'The outside wall of the house is over there,' said Cal. 'And here is a bunch of shelving in the linen closet of the bathroom, and the other side is tiled. The best way out is probably through the ceiling!'

Ruth helped him make a heap of the remaining clothing and other articles in the room. When he stood on this he could just reach the ceiling with his pocket knife in hand. Rapidly, he twisted the blade against the rough plaster. They shielded their faces against the fine shower that drifted down.

'It'll take you forever,' protested Ruth, 'if you drill enough holes that way to get through.'

'I don't intend to.' Cal continued twisting, while his arms began to ache with the awkward exertion. He stopped to rest for a moment.

'I wonder why we didn't suspect Ole before,' said Cal. 'His efforts to discredit Jorgasnovara when I first came – the breakdown of the plant as soon as he took over. Obviously, he arranged that firing to incite the union. We should have known.'

165

'We couldn't have,' said Ruth. 'We didn't have the data. He and Jorgasnovara both belong to races of supermen. Either of them could twist us around their fingers. All they need of us is manpower. Otherwise, we're nothing to either of them but chessmen to be won or lost by chance.'

'Jorgasnovara isn't that way.'

'Personally, no – but his race is of that attitude. We never had a chance.'

Cal resumed the slow drilling. At last the blade pierced the plaster board backing and went all the way through to free space in the attic beyond. He made the hole as large as he could with the knife and then lifted the metal clothes pole out of its sockets. He forced this upward against the hole he had made and twisted from side to side.

Chunks of plaster began to fall. Cal withdrew the pole and forced it upward against one edge of the small hole. A sizable chunk of plaster cracked and slid to the floor.

He stood on the pile of articles again and hung on the edge of broken plaster with all his weight. A two foot square broke loose.

'That does it.'

With one foot on the doorknob and the other against the back wall of the closet he wedged himself upward until he could draw his body through the hole to the attic.

'Stand on the pile of junk,' he called to Ruth. 'I can pull you up.'

She gave him her hand. In a few moments they were sitting together on the edge of the joists breathing hard and covered with plaster dust. In the sunlight streaming through the ventilation louvres they caught a glimpse of each other and laughed shakily.

After a brief rest, Cal reached over and raised the trap door in the ceiling of the bathroom. He jumped down and helped Ruth through the opening. Silently, they listened for sounds elsewhere in the house, but there were none.

The nauseating odor of the Guarra agents was still present, but fainter than before. The house was a shambles in the wake of Ole's departure, but no one was in it except themselves.

'What shall we do now?' said Ruth. 'Do you suppose they have left Earth?'

'If they didn't smash up the interocitor Ole had here we'll call Jorgasnovara. Maybe there's a way to stop them.'

They went to the rear bedroom which Ole had used as a study and the interocitor was still there and intact.

Cal adjusted the controls as they put on the headpieces for direct mental communication with the Llannan Engineer. For a moment the machine buzzed with the random noise of its thermionic elements. Then abruptly it cleared, and into the minds of Ruth and Cal there came a desperate cry of extreme agony.

'Cal, help me! Help me – wherever you are!' It was the cry of Jorgasnovara, the Llannan Engineer.

21

Almost instantly, upon that frantic cry from the Llannan, Cal understood the thing he had never recognized before. The purpose of the interocitor.

The instrument was not a mere communication device as he had been told. It was a weapon. An incredible weapon by which one mind could reach out and seize another to twist it, guide it, or destroy it.

Instinctively, Cal understood the strength of that terrible weapon as he witnessed its use. It could reach through force fields and armor plate that no radiation engines could destroy. This was the supreme Llannan weapon, and now the Guarra had seized it for their own, and were destroying the Llannan capacity to produce it.

A thousand awry factors suddenly fell into place. He understood the desperate Llannan need of interocitors, the Guarran theft of the instrument and sabotage.

He understood because he felt it. Felt the force of the weapon being directed against Jorgasnovara now by the Guarra agents.

But he was seized with a moment of panic as that cry came from the Llannan. He knew nothing of how to operate the machine as a weapon, and then he looked deeper, penetrating the Engineer's mind, sending out the questions and finding the answers almost as rapidly as if they were his own thoughts.

There were added circuits here, circuits which had not been put in on the assembly line. They had been made on some other world for addition to the Earth-made instruments in order to make these great weapons out of them.

Cal was one with Jorgasnovara, and Ruth joined him. They understood the meanings and operations of those additional circuits. And in the same instant they felt the flood of terrible force being hurled by the Guarra from somewhere out in space.

Cal saw Ruth pale before the onslaught. He motioned her away, but she shook her head and remained to add her strength to that of Cal and Jorgasnovara.

A wave of gratitude swelled from the mind of the Llannan. He poured out instructions directing them to let him guide their concerted attack. They agreed to follow his lead.

Alone, the machine was useless. Powered by the direct impulses of the human mind, it was like a giant amplifier multiplying the telepathic and telekinetic powers a billion fold and hurling them against the enemy.

Cal waded out into the sea of fire, but there had to be more than mere passive resistance to that flood. It had to be turned back and sent upon the Guarra, and he could not force it from him.

'It's not Ole!' Jorgasnovara said savagely.

And Cal understood. He had thought still of the Ole he had known at college, his room mate who had borrowed ties and shirts and girls. He shut out that remembrance and thought of the Ole who would attack from behind, hoping to kill. He understood then what was required to operate the interocitor weapon.

It was powered by the desire of the operator. That desire had to be for the death of the enemy. In Cal and in Ruth that desire had never been present until this moment.

Jorgasnovara helped them. He showed them what Earth would be like when the Guarra came – and for the moment they forgot there was no preventing that coming. He showed the flames sweeping round the world.

'You can't stop that,' he reminded them. 'But you can stop those who have helped bring it about. Kill them!'

They fled forth on wings of fire. They were aware of the interior of the Guarra ship. Cal understood fully the thing that Ole was, and the aspirations of the alien Guarra mind.

He hurled himself upon his former friend. Ole laughed and a livid flame sprang at Cal, throwing him down with its searing wave. He gasped amid the suffocating fire and for an instant tried to tear himself from the machine.

There was a taunting ease in the effort of Ole. The Guarra trio worked as a team with skills established by experience.

Cal knew it could not be matched. Then there was a new and deeper contact with the mind of the Llannan.

'This is it, Cal and Ruth,' said Jorgasnovara quietly. 'Follow me closely. Let me lead you, and give me all the strength you have.'

Cal had no time to wonder what the Llannan planned. Immediately, his outpouring of force battered down and washed away the wall that the Guarra had built. Cal and Ruth were carried along and added to it with all their beings.

The attack struck with living flame against the vessel in which the aliens moved. Cal had a vision of the interior again. He saw Ole and the scaly creatures. There was a moment's insight into the mind of Ole, and an instant of pity for him who had been his friend for so long. But pity died with that insight. Cal saw that in this moment of death there was no regret in Ole. His purpose had not changed. The purpose of death to all who opposed the Guarra.

The vision cut off, and Cal retreated knowing that somewhere high above the Earth a molten ball of flame plummeted to destruction.

He stood in silence and darkness then, utterly alone in all the universe. At last he opened his eyes and took off the headpiece of the interocitor. Beside him, Ruth was slumped on the floor in exhaustion. Her face was white and bitter as she looked up and slowly removed her own headpiece.

'We've got to get Jorgasnovara,' she said. 'We've got to see what happened to him.'

There had been a separation of the three of them at the moment of the vessel's destruction. Cal turned to the panel and called, but the Llannan made no answer.

Ruth got to her feet. 'Come on. We've got to hurry.'

They left the house and went out to the car. The landscape about them seemed a dim reality overshadowed by the nightmare through which they had just passed.

They drove between the neat rows of houses again to the administration building. There, they raced up the steps and through the corridor leading to Jorgasnovara's office.

Cal hesitated a moment before the closed door. Ruth brushed past him and twisted the knob impulsively. Against the far wall was mounted the interocitor, and at its base lay the inert figure of the Llannan Engineer.

The massive form was lying prone upon the floor. Cal and Ruth turned him gently over. He was still breathing, but something seemed to have gone out of him, something carrying all but a fraction of his life.

The great cranium seemed even more cadaverous. The skin was waxy on the hand that clutched impulsively at Cal's sleeve.

'Maybe it wasn't worth it,' he murmured. 'We could have let him get away. But I hated him! I knew that one of them was in our midst, but I didn't know it was Ole until now.'

'We've got to get help for you,' said Ruth.

Jorgasnovara stopped her with a wave of his hand. 'No. There is no help for one who is the victor in such an interocitor contest as I am. One can fight but a single such battle. As in all war, he who wins is also the vanquished.'

Cal understood. He had felt it. The very life substance of Jorgasnovara being converted into pure energy and hurled through space to destroy the Guarran spies.

'You have to go, now – ' said Jorgasnovara, looking from one to the other of them. 'Only you are left to go before the Council and plead for Earth as I intended to do.

'You were right. Earth does not deserve to be left to the mercy of the Guarra. Perhaps I have learned to think too much like an Earthman in the time I have been here. But I had planned to plead with the Council to defend Earth.

'Now I cannot go. Take my papers. Go before the Llanna and show them the things I believed. Tell them I believed that perhaps a war cannot be fought with justice by a machine, after all. That it takes heart, and courage, and faith. These are strange words. They will not wholly understand them, but you can explain. That is the thing you must do – help them understand once again what compassion means, for they have been at war so long in its defense that they scarcely understand it anymore.

'The ship will be here as I promised. I want them to take me back to my home world. I will not be alive when they come. You will have to do this for me, Cal and Ruth. I wish that you – '

The sentence was not finished. Slowly, the great head turned to one side, and Cal felt the life go out of the hand that still held him by the arm.

They stared for a long moment at the dead form before they dared look at each other again. Then they rose from beside the body and went out of the building into the sunlight.

Cal held his wife's hand and looked across the familiar desert. The gray and purple mountains were vague beyond the copper haze in the sky.

It may be the last time, he thought. Maybe this is the last time that we will ever see it, but there is no choice. Jorgasnovara gave them none. Their own decision long ago gave them none.

They saw Warner later in the afternoon to discuss arrangements for leaving and caring for Jorgasnovara's body. The death of his leader seemed to have done something to Warner. It had put a shell about him. A cracked and brittle shell that left Cal with the feeling that the Llannan regretted his whole part in the Terrestrian project.

Packing, that afternoon, was like something done in a dream. They inventoried all their possessions, and estimated all possible needs in the long future and began assembling nearly everything they owned.

At once they saw the futility of trying to prepare for indefinite existence on the unknown world to which they were going.

'We're going to live there, so we'll have to use what is available there. Let's cut this down,' said Cal.

They ended by taking a minimum, what they could carry in a half dozen suitcases. When they were through, it was still mid-afternoon, and the ship would not come until midnight. Warner was taking care of the body of Jorgasnovara, and there was nothing of importance left for Cal and Ruth to do.

They went out of the house and over to the plant where they walked through the empty corridors and passed the assembly lines, still half demolished. They encountered only an occasional watchman or maintenance engineer.

The plant would become a great mystery, Cal thought. The salaries of these men would stop, and suddenly there would be found no one at all in authority over the plant. The Government would investigate and its agents would wonder what strange sabotage was brewed here. They would if there were time enough for such wonder before the Guarra legions swept it from the face of the Earth.

He wondered why he kept thinking with such complete certainty that this was going to happen. If he had so completely accepted this in his own mind there was no use going before the Llannan Council. He would have no chance at all to make a plea for Earth.

In the hot afternoon sunlight, he tried to shake that conviction out of him. He tried to let the clean light of the desert burn the infection of that thought from his mind.

Walking beside him, Ruth felt the tensions as he struggled to shed his apprehensions. They were not in her, yet she knew she could not help him. She could not absorb his conviction or drive it out of him.

For herself, she knew that this land was never going to be swept by the Guarra fire. These buildings and these people were not going to vanish in a puff of flame at the whim of the invader. It would not have helped Cal for her to say these things. Yet she knew that this was the way it was going to be. They were going to turn aside the Guarran horde.

She did not know how this was going to come about. She only knew that it was going to be so.

22

The spaceship came at midnight. It landed at the same place, at the great doors of the shipping platform, where they had first seen it in all its mystery and grandeur.

As they went aboard this time, Ruth thought of that day in Los Angeles when Cal had said, '*I want to see space.*' She wondered what he was thinking now as they were embarking upon this first journey to deep space.

There was no joy in his face, only grim determination. He seemed wholly oblivious to the journey they were about to undertake.

The Commander of the ship welcomed them, and was saddened by the news of Jorgasnovara's death. That news seemed to pervade the whole vessel within moments of its landing and made of it a funeral barge.

As they heard the faint thud of the hatches being sealed, Cal and Ruth sat by the port of their stateroom. They saw the Earth begin its long retreat, without feeling the effects of the vast acceleration. In a matter of minutes, it seemed, the moon swung past their vision and they knew they were beyond its orbit.

Jorgasnovara had never told them clearly where the center of government of the Llannan Council lay. It was a voyage of sixteen Earth days, the Commander later told them. In the chart room he pointed out the great trajectory over which the ship was hurtling at many times the speed of light.

He made no comment on the purpose of their journey. They had presented Jorgasnovara's papers to him as the Engineer had instructed. As the journey progressed, Cal felt that a faint, invisible wall between him and the Llanna was slowly thickening.

Its increasing pressure forced him to attempt a way through it. He cornered Warner in the chart room when they were halfway out.

'Why don't any of you believe Ruth and I should try to carry out the mission Jorgasnovara planned?'

Warner's face lost some of the austerity it had held since his leader's death. 'We can understand you, and why you would want to do such a thing. It is Jorgasnovara whom we do not understand. He knew the insignificance of Earth in the broad scope of our military plans. Why he should have allowed his sentimentality to overwhelm him in the face of that knowledge is beyond our understanding.'

'I'll bet you could understand it if it were your own world that was being overrun,' said Ruth with fury in her voice.

'I have seen that very thing,' said Warner quietly. 'Thirty years ago. I watched while my own planet was burned and our fleet stood helplessly by.'

'I'm sorry,' said Ruth humbly. 'I didn't know.'

'We're glad you're with us,' said Warner. 'We will make a place for you, but we wish you would give up this foolish and vain hope. It can only lead to disappointment and perhaps the establishment of enmity between us if that disappointment is great enough.'

'Perhaps,' said Cal. 'But we have to try.'

It gave Cal no overall understanding of the Llannan military problem, but he began to feel an understanding of what it was like to be a people who had been at war all their lives. He could understand just a little how they could be struggling for the survival of good will among sentient creatures of the universe and yet consider the sacrifice of a world as a small thing in itself.

The landing of the vessel was made on Jorgasnovara's home world. It was, as he had told them, a place not unlike Earth. The light of its sun burned down with familiar warmth and color. The grasp of its gravity and the texture of its sod beneath their feet were no different, and the air they breathed might have been blowing through a cool familiar valley upon Earth itself.

They watched the solemn rites that accompanied the chemical dissolution of Jorgasnovara's body and its dispersal into the seas as was customary among his people.

For the first time they realized how high he must have been in the Council of the Llanna, and how revered on his home world. They were called upon time after time to repeat the story of his final struggle with the Guarra agents. It would become a legend to add to the endless annals of heroic deeds accumulated by this people in their long struggle for security.

Warner took it upon himself to act as their host and ambassador, as if recognizing that he had been unnecessarily harsh during the first days of the journey. The day after Jorgasnovara's rites he came to them in the plain quarters that had been assigned to them.

'The papers have been presented to the Council,' he said. 'They have accepted Jorgasnovara's report, and have agreed to listen to your message.'

Cal had already discovered that the governing body of the Llannan worlds was an almost unbelievable thing. The Council was not concentrated on any one planet nor was it composed of any single race.

There were representatives of more than a hundred races. Each met in their own Council chambers on planets of many galaxies. These chambers were linked by the faster than light communications that welded them as closely as if they had met about a single conference table.

Cal understood that he would meet with only a comparatively small sub-council. There was scarcely any problem of sufficient magnitude to demand the attention of the whole Council, but his would be acted upon by the larger body, upon recommendation by the sub-council.

Warner led him through the corridors of the Council building in the center of the city. There, high on an upper floor, he entered the local chambers where a score of representatives of this world were seated about a table.

Overhead, and on panels surrounding them were the intricate communication devices linking them with numerous and similar chambers in other galaxies where the rulers of the Llanna would give brief audience to his plea for Earth.

Those about the table were as man-like as Jorgasnovara had been. For this he was grateful. If he had been among a Council of nightmare creatures like the two Guarra, he could not have endured it, he thought.

The group leader spoke from the head of the table. His voice was kindly as Jorgasnovara's had been, but it carried the same incisive determination, an assurance that his audience would be brief but courteously heard – and decided with a finality from which there would be no appeal.

They waited then for Cal to speak.

'I have asked to come before you,' he said slowly, 'to make a personal appeal for my planet. You know the nature of that appeal. You have the papers of your agent, Jorgasnovara, before you.

'Through him, you prevailed upon us to cooperate in the manufacture of interocitors and other instruments. Now, through the accident of the Guarra attack, which this assistance drew upon us, you have abandoned us to the enemy.

'I protest this abandonment!'

178

Cal shifted his eyes about the group. They were listening politely – and with pre-determined decision. He could read it in their faces, the admission that his cause was just, and resignation to its hopelessness.

His voice grew edgy with anger. He checked himself, and went on more deliberately. 'I was told by Jorgasnovara that the great cause for which you have sustained this conflict is the preservation of cooperative, sentient life in the universe. I represent two and a half billion members of one species of that life.

'Almost none of them have any knowledge of this attack which is coming. I was led to involve them upon the assurance that Earth lay far beyond the bounds of any Guarran activity. By deception, we were led into cooperation in the initial belief that we were promoting peace. When we discovered it was an effort of war we continued that cooperation in the belief that your goals were righteous and deserved our support.

'Your betrayal of our cooperative effort cannot be overbalanced by ten thousand victories. If you feel no obligation to defend this island Earth against the unexpected Guarran invasion you are not worthy to seek the goal you are fighting for. You are worthy only of defeat, and if you betray my people to the Guarra you are already defeated.

'You do not understand the meaning of your goal. You do not understand that no victory, however great, can compensate for a single betrayal of those who have an investment of trust in you.

'I ask for a defense of my planet Earth by the forces of the Llannan Council!'

Abruptly, Cal finished and returned to his seat. Right and left, about that circle of faces surrounding the table, he saw no politeness now. There was agitation in every face, but he could not read the expressions. There were one or two short whispered conferences, but most of the members were silent and grim.

He sensed the similar results that he had produced on the many other worlds of the Llannan Council. Presently, the evaluations of all of them would be transmitted to the central computer and swiftly integrated into a single final answer.

A small light glowed in the table panel in front of the group leader. He punched at the small keyboard there and his eyes scanned the sheet that appeared. After a long silence, he arose slowly and began speaking.

'Cal Meacham, of Earth, it is a momentous indictment which you bring against the Llannan Council for their interference in the affairs of your world.

'We came to you originally because the interocitor is our prime weapon, and of all the races with which we have contact, yours is one of the best equipped to assist in the production of the weapon. You understand that your production was but a drop of the total we required, but it was to have been increased many fold and become one of our major supply centers. This, the Guarra knew through their agent who infiltrated into the project.

'For your help we are grateful. We wish with all our beings that there might be a way for justice to answer your request. But there is none.

'We have learned by long and very sad experience that war cannot be fought by whim or even by mercy. It can be fought only by cold computation which can predict accurately the outcome of any projected action. We can predict the outcome of a retreat from your section. The defense of Earth cannot be predicted except as a random factor totally unrelated to the final objectives. To send a large force on such a mission would expose it to defeat for a purpose wholly unrelated to the ultimate goal of our military maneuvers.

'We know the emotions with which you accompany this charge against us. To this we must be blind. Perhaps you are right – that we have already lost the goal. We learned long ago that it may have been lost at the very moment when creatures first essayed such a conflict as this one in which we and our ancestors have been engaged. We do not know. We know only that it is to go on, even at the risk of the goals for which it is being fought.

'You do not understand, of course, the military requirements which have led to the decision to abandon your island, Earth. We grant, if you wish it, the privilege of examining our military computers by which these decisions are made. We would grant, even, that if you could better the ultimate plan and show how military expediency could be served by the defense of Earth, that such defense might be undertaken. But we know, of course, that this is an impossibility, and we do not place such a burden upon you.

'All we can say is that your request cannot be granted, Cal Meacham of Earth.'

23

He returned to the house where Ruth waited and reported what had happened. She remained as still and silent as a portrait while he told her the words of the group leader.

It was like turning around in the middle of a life and discovering all that had gone before was a dream, she thought.

'There's another answer, somewhere, somehow – ' she said. There was movement only of her lips as she continued staring through the window at the distant landscape that might have been of Earth – almost.

'We ought to go back,' said Cal. He was staring out the window, too. 'If they would take us back, we ought to go. We have no right to stay here.'

'What was it they said, Cal – That if you could find a military reason for defending Earth they would do it? That's our answer. You've got to find a military advantage in it for them. A real one – or make one up! It doesn't matter anymore!'

She turned suddenly, her eyes blazing. 'They tricked us. They lied to us. It doesn't matter anymore what we do to them! Find a lie that they will believe – and make them save Earth!'

He watched her slump forward, her hands over her face. He listened to her cry without moving to comfort her.

You find a lie – *You* – Even Ruth knew that the responsibility was his. He couldn't put it anywhere else. He tried to think that it was as much the fault of the scores of other engineers and workmen who had fallen for the Peace Engineers' deception. But it wasn't. The Guarra had kept them in check, and all the Llannan emissaries. Only when Cal had tried to persuade Jorgasnovara there was one proper way to get the production he wanted had the Guarra taken the steps to attack.

The offer of the Council was a farce, of course. He could not hope to beat their vast computers in thinking out a war plan. If the computers could find no military expediency in defending Earth, he could not. The only grounds were those of mercy and justice. And you couldn't put those into a computer!

He crossed the room and sat down in a deep chair. He closed his eyes and looked down the years ahead of them. There was nothing. The Llanna wouldn't return them to Earth, of course.

'The only thing we can do is volunteer for some kind of assignment to help them carry on,' he said. 'It's the only way we can hope to make up even a little bit.'

She watched his face misshapen by regret. His defeat had taken him completely from her. He was like a hollow man now and would never be anything else if he found no answer.

She felt relief after her tears. She wished that Cal would break, too, and let the dammed up misery flow out of him. But she knew he would not.

'You've got to try what they offered.' She approached and sat down beside him. 'Maybe it's a wild, foolish chance, but so was this whole trip. They gave you their word. Maybe they would not break it if you could show them *something*.'

Later in the day Warner came to see them again. Cal asked about the possibility of going back. Warner shook his head. 'You knew this was a one way trip when you started.'

'Will you let us visit the computers, as the Council suggested?' asked Ruth.

Warner smiled faintly. 'That was an idle suggestion, you understand. There is nothing you could do to alter the general program of the war.'

'You'll take us there?' Ruth persisted.

'If that's what you want.'

The great building of the military computing engines was one of a multitude on many planets. It housed receptor and transmission units. The computer and library were actually on another planet, but all data and computations were available to each world through similar units as this one.

They went about the many floors of the building. Warner patiently showed them the intricate workings. At first Cal was almost indifferent to those things and Ruth did most of the questioning. But in the central planning room where the final digestion of data was interpreted on the great star charts he took increased interest.

He saw a duplicate of the chart Jorgasnovara had shown him days before. He saw how the plan of action and the battle lines had shifted – closer to his own galaxy. He wondered exactly why the computers had given out the answer that the line should not be held beyond that galaxy. Abruptly, the whole machinery of the computer took on meaning. There *was* something he wanted to know here!

Even if Earth could not be saved, he wanted to know why. He bent over the chart and began an examination of the equations adjacent to it. With the help of the Llannan technician in charge, he began tracing his way through, conversing by means of the interpreting instrument provided for him.

He became oblivious to the presence of Ruth and Warner. Only hours later did he realize what he had done, that Ruth and Warner were no longer with him. In that time, however, he had established close communication with the Llannan technician, Rakopt.

When he reached home he was still preoccupied. Ruth asked, 'How much longer is there – ?'

'About two weeks.' The question irritated him. He was restless during dinner and avoided Ruth's glance. After the meal he rose.

'I'm going down there again for a few hours. You won't mind?'

She shook her head, holding back the questions that were on her lips. She dared not ask if he had found anything.

He was there the next day, and shortly, all his waking hours were being spent at the computer building. He was restless when he came home, and slept fitfully during the night. There was something that Ruth could sense building to the point of detonation within him, but she dared not risk setting it off by asking questions.

The fifth night after his initial visit to the computer, Cal did not get to bed at all when he came home. He slumped in the deep chair by the window that looked out over the sparsely lit city in the night. Ruth put a robe about her and came out to sit by him.

'Can I help?' she said.

He turned as if seeing her for the first time in several days. He smiled wanly. 'Time,' he said. 'If there were time, something might show up. I can see something, but I don't know what it is. Something is wrong with the whole basis of Llannan calculations. I can't put my finger on it. And there's only another week – '

'How about a good sleep, and putting the whole thing out of your mind for one night?'

'No.' He leaned his head back and stared up at the ceiling. 'There was something that Jorgasnovara was always saying – predictability. He had a phobia about things that were not predictable. On the plant dispersal plan, you remember, he wouldn't take a chance without getting a check on the predictability of its results. Without a crystal ball, he was lost. I've noticed the same thing about the rest of them here. Nobody will so much as spit without being able to predict within three decimal places where they will hit.'

He sat up suddenly. 'That's it! That's the answer to their whole failure in this war. They've got to throw away their crystal balls! If I could only make them see it – '

'I don't understand – '

He kissed her suddenly and stood up. 'Get some sleep, honey. I don't know when I'll be back.'

Before he left he put in a call to Rakopt, who agreed to meet him at the computer building.

The computer was attended around the clock, but Rakopt worked days only. The young Llannan technician, however, had become so absorbed by Cal's problem that he hoped almost as much as the Earthman that the problem would be solved. But he had no understanding of how this might be done.

His eyes were eager as he met Cal in the chart room. 'Have you got it?' he said.

'If I understand your operations thoroughly enough,' said Cal, 'the purpose of the computer is chiefly that of prediction.'

'Of course,' said Rakopt. 'That is obvious.'

'You predict what the Guarra will do on the basis of their strength, and also what you should do to best counter and attack their forces?'

'Yes.'

'But the Guarra also have computers.'

Rakopt nodded. 'Theirs are very good. It is almost a battle of computers rather than armies. And that is the

186

reason why no non-computable factors are allowed to enter as far as we are able to control them.'

'But what do you do to lower your own predictability to the Guarra?' said Cal. 'If they know the logic of your computers, the strength of your forces, and your ultimate goals they know almost exactly what you will do from day to day.'

'We try to keep their knowledge of our forces as incomplete as possible,' said Rakopt. 'What else can we do?'

'Throw away your computers!' said Cal.

Warner was surprised by Cal's request for an immediate audience with the Council again, but he agreed to arrange it. Cal had no sleep that night. He went home to shave for the first time in four days, and to eat and change clothes.

'You come along this time,' he said to Ruth. 'We've either got it or we haven't.'

The Council chamber was filled with an atmosphere of unbelieving expectancy. No one in the room or in any of the galaxy-distant chambers believed that Cal would ask for another appearance. There was unrest mingled with irritation that he should approach them with matters already decided.

'I have studied the history of your wars,' he said in beginning. 'For a long time you have been engaged in a calculated retreat before the Guarran forces. Retreat is not victory. I know what your long-term goals are, of course, but even though you face your goals you do not approach them by walking backwards.

'From Jorgasnovara I learned the one thing the Llanna demand of themselves and the universe – predictability. You even demand it of your enemies, the Guarra. With your great computers, you determine exactly what a course should be in view of the known forces and objectives.

'And the Guarra do the same. They predict you almost down to the seventeenth decimal place. And you carefully oblige them by carrying forth as expected!'

The group leader interrupted. 'If you please, our time is limited.'

'All right, then. Here is what you have done: You line yourselves up like sitting ducks with your incredibly accurate predicting computers and the Guarra pick you off at will. For a generation you have operated with a technique in which defeat is inevitable!'

A half dozen Councilors were on their feet. 'We have no obligation to endure this nonsense – !'

The group leader motioned for order. 'We have promised to hear this out,' he reminded them.

'It should have been obvious to you long ago,' said Cal, 'why you have been in constant retreat.'

'The Guarran forces have been measurably greater,' said the Councilor on his left. 'We have been forced to be prudent with our own resources.'

'That is sheer nonsense!' said Cal. 'The secret is that the Guarra know how to break the predictability equations. Think about it: You were all ready to set up a major supply point on Earth. At *no* point until the very last did you know that the Guarra were going to attack. Where were your fine computers then?

'I remember the dismay with which Jorgasnovara told me of the shift in the line. I thought he was concerned with Earth, then. Now I know what a blow it was to him to contemplate this surprise move of the Guarra.

'But why did your computers fail to show you that Earth would be attacked if you set up an interocitor center there?'

'There are many factors – ' said the group leader.

'But the most important factor is that the Guarra are better computermen than you. They know how to deliberately make themselves unpredictable to your machines. It has happened before. It will happen again as long as you, yourselves, remain so completely predictable.

'Their method is to operate under certain circumstances by a completely random thrust. Such is their strike toward Earth – random. The attack had no predicating factors. Jorgasnovara believed it was due to the failure of the Guarran agents to hold down production without an attack. Such was not true. I felt it was not a valid answer then. I know now that it was not. The Guarra picked Earth as their target at complete random.

'They'll do it again, combining it with brute force attacks against your main fleets, but in the end it will be the random attacks that win – for the Guarra.'

The Councilors were silent, sitting as if sudden recognition of a long dreaded ghost had come upon them. Cal knew that they sensed the truth of what he said. In their great pride of accomplishment in precision warfare, they had not looked to this ghost that haunted them.

'We've seen it happen on Earth,' said Cal gently now. 'Troops trained and drilled and marched through forests to be slaughtered by random attacking aborigines. When you fight such an enemy you use his own tactics against him.'

'And that is – ' said the group leader.

'Send every ship you can spare to the defense of the failing line. Yes, defend my Earth. The Guarra *know* you won't. Your computers tell you not to, and they know it. So do it. I don't know if you'll win. Intelligence is too incomplete to show the balance of forces available. But one thing you will do is throw off the Guarran predictability and let them know they've been in one hell of a fight. And that, I assure you, will bring your own final victory much closer to possibility. You will no longer be sitting ducks, no longer finely drilled troops marching through a forest of random fighters!'

The hours that passed next were long. It was night again when Warner finally brought the news. Rakopt was with him and the eyes of both men were glowing with excitement.

'The Council has agreed,' said Warner. 'Earth will be defended.' Then he extended his hand and took Cal's and Ruth's warmly, in turn. 'And I'm very glad,' he said.

Ruth cried then. She put her head against Cal's shoulder and let the long days of apprehension release.

'We won,' she sobbed. 'I knew it would be this way – '

'No,' Warner reminded her soberly. 'We haven't won, but we've got a chance now, and maybe Cal is right – the whole war may be nearer its end because of this.'

Word went out to the fleets that night. Ships were transferred to the new battle zone. On one of these Ruth and Cal and Warner were picked up.

Through the port, while the battleship was still in primary drive, Cal and Ruth watched the receding home of Jorgasnovara as it disappeared among the pinpoints of light. Whether the battle were won or lost, he supposed they would not see it again.

With the shifting to secondary drive, the whole star-scape vanished and he turned away. He thought of all he had done since the Llanna had first approached him. He wondered if he would do it again the same way. And suddenly he knew that he would. Like it or not, Earth was a member of the community of worlds. That there was no established commerce, and the fact that Earthmen did not know of the existence of the Llanna or the Guarra made no difference whatever. What happened between the Llanna and the Guarra now would affect the destiny of unborn generations of Earthmen. The present generation should have a word as to what that destiny might be.

The Llanna had made foolish blunders. They had fought the war in their own set way so long that they had forgotten there were other ways. They were on the road to defeat. Of this, Cal was certain.

Whether his introduction of guerrilla fighting tactics in space war would change that, he didn't know, but at least it would make the Llanna less vulnerable.

Ruth watched him from the chair by the port. 'Is it the way you thought it would be, as fine and wonderful as you hoped?' she said.

'What?'

'Space, that you wanted to see so badly.'

He glanced at the port, blackened by the secondary drive. 'I guess I haven't had time to think much about it.' His thoughts scanned the romantic yearning he'd once had toward the stars, the aching urge with which he had once looked up at the sky. It would be good to look up at it again – from Earth – he thought.

'Must be getting old for that sort of thing,' he said. 'I think I'm ready for the little house with a lawn around it – and kids riding tricycles on the sidewalk.'